"The main focus here is on how people can become successful while being true to their core values. The illustrative stories are riveting as Peter constructs the way for business careers to be human transformations. His 'coincidences' in what he calls the 'Web of Life' surprise and delight. It is heartwarming to see someone who has met the challenges at the top of the business game write an honest portrait to inspire others in their personal quest."

DR. GEORGE H. WESTACOTT,
Former Dean of School of Management,
State University of New York at Binghamton

"Peter Kash has written a book that is fun to read and filled with sound practical advice for aspiring entrepreneurs. He inspires confidence and hope that ordinary folks can make their entrepreneurial dreams come true. Peter's 'been there/done that' stories provide meaningful lessons and road maps for those who want to create entrepreneurial ventures."

DR. RUDY LAMONE, FOUNDER AND CHAIRMAN
Dingman Center for Entrepreneurship
Former Dean of the Robert H. Smith
School of Business, University of Maryland

"After reading *Make Your Own Luck* I am tempted to give up preaching. I could pass out the book to my parishioners with a note saying, 'This is the message.' Call it faith in God or faith in the web of life; we have every reason to hope, strive, and trust. This is what people need to hear and believe; and this book presents that message with simple clarity and the force of authenticity."

THE REV. SUSAN AUCHINCLOSS
Rector, St. John's Episcopal Church
New City, New York

"*Make Your Own Luck* is an inspirational account of a man's successful journey through life and career. Peter Kash shares his experiences and those of other successful businesspeople and teaches us how to transform coincidence into opportunity and failure into success. His easy-to-follow tips for enhancing one's career and leading a more satisfying life are important lessons for all young people searching for insights about how to conduct their working lives in positive and constructive ways."

ARTHUR L. CENTONZE, PH.D.
Dean, Lubin School of Business
Pace University

"*Make Your Own Luck* is similar to my first book, *Powerful Prayers*, co-authored with Larry King. Many people we interviewed, such as Presidents Jimmy Carter and Gerald Ford, and professional athletes like Muhammed Ali had setbacks in life or in business. Peter's book acts as a facilitator to help you find your place in the web of life."

RABBI IRWIN KATSOF
Co-Author *Powerful Prayers* with Larry King
Executive Director - The Jerusalem Fund

"When first reading Peter's book, I thought it would be about business but he embodied the philosophy of Martial Arts: HARMONY with one-self and their environment as well as PERSEVERANCE. I recommend this book to all athletes, amateur and professional."

SHIHAN MOTI HORENSTEIN
World Super Heavyweight
Muay Thai Karate Champion 6th Degree Blackbelt

Make Your Own Luck

Success Tactics
You Won't Learn in B-School

Make Your Own Luck

Success Tactics
You Won't Learn in B-School

Peter Morgan Kash
with Tom Monte

Prentice
Hall Press

Library of Congress Cataloging-in-Publication Data

Kash, Peter
  Make your own luck: Success tatics you'll never learn in business school / by Peter
Kash and Tom Monte.
     p. cm.
  ISBN 0-7352-0224-9 (cloth)
     1. Career development —Psychological aspects. 2. Success—Psychological aspects.
  3. Success in business. 4. Life skills 5. Fortune 6. Chance. I. Monte, Tom. II. Title.

  HF5381 .K3647 2002
  650.14–dc21   2001036426

Printed in the United States of America

10   9   8   7   6   5   4   3   2   1

ISBN 0-7352-0224-9

Acquisitions editor: Tom Power
Production editor: Jacqueline Roulette
Interior design: Robyn Beckerman
Page layout: Shelly Carlucci

ATTENTION: CORPORATIONS AND SCHOOLS

Prentice Hall Press books are available at quantity discounts with bulk purchase for
educational, business, or sales promotional use. For information, please write to:
Prentice Hall Direct, Special Sales, 240 Frisch Court, Paramus, NJ 07652. Please supply: title of book, ISBN, quantity, how the book will be used, date needed.

 Paramus, NJ 07652

http://www.phpress.com

*To my parents, Leona and Robert, for not allowing
the word* can't *in my vocabulary.*

*To my wife and best friend, Donna,
for sharing the ride of life with me.*

Acknowledgements

This book would not have been written without the guidance, assistance, and support from many people, some of whom I feel compelled to thank in writing. First, I thank my co-author Tom Monte, whose gift for expressing thoughts and visions on paper is uncanny; our agent Linda Roghaar who helped us find the right home for our book; and special thanks to our editor, Tom Power, and publisher, Gene Brissie, who shared our vision and the belief that this book could help people.

Lindsay Rosenwald, M.D., my boss, partner, and friend for 13 years, allowed me the freedom to explore other endeavors and dreams. My executive assistant, Elizabeth Allen, helped me manage a worldwide travel and lecture schedule, while trying to write this book. Elizabeth deserves my utmost praise and thanks for her abilities and patience. I am grateful to colleagues and friends in my office who picked up some of my workload, especially Jillian Hoffman, Martin Kratchman, Josh Kazam, Fred Mermelstein, Ph.D., Mark Rogers, M.D., David Tanen, J. D. and Michael Weiser, M.D., Ph.D.

I thank my earliest mentors, Robert Harris and Howard Schain, who, while I was still a teenager, tried to teach me compassion and a broader perspective on life. I also want to thank my first managers, Charlie Murphy, Jr. and Art Carine, Jr. at E.F. Hutton, who taught me about integrity and responsibility; and Kenton Wood and Morty Davis, two old friends who gave me my start in venture capital. Mr. Chico Sabbah taught me the gift of charity. Also, I want to thank Dr. Scott Bernstein, Dr. Steve Blechman, Dr. Ken Pearlman, Dr. Robert Klein and Dr. Yuichi Iwaki, a renowned transplant surgeon, for their friendship over the last fifteen years. I would also like to thank Dr. Chris Michelson, chief of spinal surgery at Columbia Presbyterian Hospital, helped me walk again after I ruptured my L5S1 disc; and Dr. Mark Seem, my acupuncturist, opened a whole new world of medicine for me.

I want to thank my students for teaching me more than they could have possibly learned from me. Lastly, I thank my wife, confidante, and best friend Donna, and my children, Jared, Colby and Shantal, who had to miss a few play dates and events in order to make this book a reality.

Contents

CHAPTER 4
THE ANATOMY OF A DEAL   93

CHAPTER 5
HOW TO GET THE
ANSWER YOU WANT   115

Introduction

Most people enter the workforce with a single priority in mind: financial reward. As we move along in our careers, we eventually realize that we need more than a paycheck to truly feel satisfied and fulfilled in our work. As Maslow stated, once our survival is taken care of, other needs awaken. Sooner or later, we find ourselves wanting our work to be the medium through which we develop our talents and abilities. We realize that we need to work in an atmosphere of trust and mutual respect. We want to be recognized for our contributions, not just to the company for which we work, but also to our community. The challenges we face in our work should somehow help us become larger and more developed human beings. We want to grow in such a way that we become our best selves.

Many people respond cynically to my statement. "That's asking a little much, isn't it?" some reply.

Perhaps, I say, but it's worth remembering that your job will require about a third of your adult life, or about half of your waking hours, which means that your work will shape you in ways that go far beyond your bank account. The type of work that you do, the spirit with which you do it, and the atmosphere within your workplace, all combine to mold you into the person you will become. It's not too far-fetched to say that work is destiny, because your job will transform you.

Ask yourself if getting a paycheck is the only thing that's really important to you. If not, then ask yourself what other things in a job matter to you. If you absolutely need to express your own ideas and creativity; if you must develop your talents; if an atmosphere of trust and mutual respect is essential; if growing as a human being is a prerequisite to your happiness; and, yes, if you need to be rewarded financially in a way that is commensurate with your abilities, then these are not luxuries, but necessities for your life. You will not be truly satisfied with your life unless these needs are fulfilled. Ask yourself a simple question: What kind of person will I become if my work does not provide me with these opportunities and experiences? There's a good chance that you're not going to like the answer.

This book is a practical guide to help you realize these basic necessities in your work and career. My intention is to show you how you can turn your job into a rewarding and fulfilled life—and, in the process, become the person you want to be.

The first step in making such a change is to be clear about what you need from your work and career. The second is to know what you must do in order to fulfill those needs. In this book, I attempt to show you how you can do just that.

People argue that there is a danger in asking for too much from life, that you'll set yourself up for disappointment and failure. Actually, there's a danger in asking for too much *and* for too little. If you think small, you'll ask little of yourself and experience only small rewards. That's a formula for dissatisfaction, disappointment, and failure. If you ask for a lot, you might be dissatisfied, too, but only if you have big dreams and ask too little of yourself as you attempt to fulfill them.

Still, the real danger in life, as I see it, is not expressed by the question of whether to ask for too little or too much. That's the wrong question, because it implies that the job of your dreams can be given to you. The job of your dreams is not dropped in your lap; no one can give you the perfect job. Rather, it is created by you.

Work is a very rough outline of tasks. What matters is how well you perform those tasks, the spirit with which you do them, and how you relate to others as you do your work. Your job is created by your unique set of idiosyncratic talents and personality characteristics. Your behavior, expertise, attitudes, and spirit affect the way people relate to you. And in the process, these characteristics either create opportunities for you or close them down. Thus, a career is made—either for good or ill. You are much more in charge of your destiny than you might think.

In this book, I try to show you how to create the kind of career you truly want for your life. In effect, I am trying to provide you with a rough roadmap to the kind of destiny you want.

As I show in great detail, all of us must learn certain essential strategies in order to succeed. We must begin by realizing that opportunities usually show up in our lives as coincidences. Those coincidences are themselves presented in rather humble packaging. For example, you may meet someone quite unexpectedly who, it later turns out, offers you an opportunity that you would never have guessed possible, one that will change your life. Or, you may find yourself in a situation—at a conference, for example, or in a social gathering—in which you unexpectedly encounter someone whom you know could mean a lot to your career. In both cases, the coincidences set the stage, so to speak. It is now up to you to seize the day. In this book, I provide guidance on when to take that fateful leap and when to hold back.

"What if I fail?" people ask me. Let me put this as gently as I can: I guarantee that you will experience failure—again and again. Failure, as I point out at length in Chapter 3, is an essential experience on the path to success. The question isn't whether you will fail, but what will you do after you fail? All success is based on our actions in the wake of failure. I have studied the lives of successful people the world over. Every one of them has failed—repeatedly. Unlike many people who call themselves failures, however, these people didn't let failure keep them from succeeding.

I have a lot to say throughout the book about how to create opportunity, but two approaches are worth mentioning in advance. The first is values. The person you are is determined by your values, which in turn will determine your behavior. Your behavior will determine how you affect others, which in turn will determine the amount of opportunity people offer you. Never forget that your values show. Sooner or later, people know who you are and the values that motivate your actions.

One of the most powerful ways of generating enormous opportunity is to specialize and become an expert in a single area of your profession. Develop your knowledge and skills in a given area so that you are superior to your competition, and you will become known throughout your field. Acquiring extraordinary expertise is one of the keys to accruing both power and wealth.

A wise man once said to me, "You can have anything you want in life. All you have to do is gamble your life to get it." That was extraordinary wisdom, because he captured something fundamental about life: Everything has a price, and even if you pay the price, there is no guarantee that you'll get what you want. Life is a gamble.

The only things you have any control over are your own thoughts and actions. Yet, your thoughts and actions give you tremendous power to shape events and determine how others behave in your company. That means that the power to transform your job into the ideal job begins with you—not with your boss or your co-workers. No one else can make you an expert in what you do; no one else can make you a person of rich and lasting values. As you transform yourself into the kind of person that you respect and admire, you gradually become the person others look to for guidance and leadership.

The price of every goal—whether it is in your career, finances, or family—is time, energy, concentration, and commitment. You must give these four in order to make anything in your life grow and prosper. You have limited amounts of all four, which means you cannot spend them willy-nilly on any old thing that comes along. Life requires choices, and choices determine what you get in life. Our choices are made on the basis of what's truly important to us. Therefore, choose the things that are most important to you and give yourself—that is, give your time, energy, concentration, and commitment—to them. Chances are very good that you will get the things you want from life.

As we struggle to achieve our goals, we often forget that we are getting help from mysterious quarters of life. Opportunities arise from out of the blue that we would never have expected. These opportunities shape our careers and, in the end, determine our destiny. I do not attempt to explain the mystery behind such events, which I refer to as the web of life, because I can't. All I can do is acknowledge that it's there and show people how to make it work for them.

In this book, I have tried to show what is truly important in creating a successful and rewarding career. Indeed, I have tried to reveal some of the essentials to creating a fulfilled and happy life.

Peter Kash

Make Your Own Luck

Success Tactics
You Won't Learn in B-School

CHAPTER 1

The Magic of Coincidence

We learn wisdom from failure much more than from success.
We often discover what will do by finding out what
not to do; and probably he who never made
a mistake never made a discovery.

—Samuel Smiles

*I*n spring of 1988, I was sitting at my desk at 7:30 in the morning when the phone rang. The voice on the other end, clear, authoritative, and a bit impatient, asked for someone I didn't know. Rather than tell him that no one by that name was at this number, I asked for his name. I was following my own advice. As I tell my students at the University of Pennsylvania's Wharton School of Business, you never know who is on the other end of the line. Find out.

He gave his name and said he was the executive producer for a news program called "Financial News Network."

"Well, you've dialed the wrong number," I said, "but if you are ever looking for a knowledgeable person on the Japanese economy and biotechnology, let me know. I'll be happy to guest host a show," I said. With that I gave him my name and telephone number and hung up.

Six months later, Ellyse Newman, a producer at FNN, telephoned me, desperate that I appear on a program about the Japanese economy. Apparently the show's guest, a Japanese banker, had canceled at the last minute. I was happy to oblige. As it turned out, the show I hosted was such a hit that the network asked me to host a bi-monthly program on FNN called

"International Spotlight," which I did for about two years, until the network was bought by CNBC.

All my life I have been reaping the rewards offered in moments that we typically refer to as coincidence. I am a venture capitalist, which means I raise money to start up or support breakthrough medical technologies around the world. I specialize in biotechnology. Most of the companies I raise money for are searching for answers to the world's worst scourges—cancer, diabetes, AIDS, heart disease, infectious illnesses, and various types of genetic disorders. Over the past 20 years, my partners and I have raised a lot of money—more than $500 million. In the vast majority of cases, the return on these investments has been substantial—in some instances as much as ten- to twenty-fold. That is not to say that I haven't had my share of failures, too. As Jerry Maguire's mentor says at the end of that charming movie, I've failed as many times as I've succeeded. But as I like to tell my potential investors, if we all go broke, we'll have done it as we tried to make a better world for our children. That may sound a bit hokey, but it's what I believe. And in any case, it's true. A great many of the companies we have supported have made scientific and medical breakthroughs that have changed the world.

In addition to my work as a venture capitalist, I am also a lecturer of Entrepreneurship at the Wharton School of Business, the nation's top business college, and a visiting professor at Nihon University in Japan.

In the course of my career, I've been involved with many companies and closed a lot of deals, and I can tell you that unexpected events played an important role in the success or failure of virtually all of them. In the most successful cases, there have always been what you might call magical coincidences that offered tremendous opportunities. Recognizing the opportunities implicit in these seemingly coincidental events is one of the most important keys to success.

In this book, I'm going to show you how you can place your career on the surest path to success. The guidance I provide can work for anyone, at any career level. After more than two decades of doing business, I have found that the recommendations I outline here are fundamental truths about life—they work as effectively for young people as they do for more established leaders. They are essential to success, no matter what your nationality or educational background. In fact, they are the basis for conducting business successfully the world over. Once you make these behaviors, values, and outlook your own—that is, make them a part of your daily life—you will see every aspect of your career transformed. Indeed, they will transform your life.

The first of these behaviors seems very simple, at least on the surface. It is the art of recognizing opportunity when it appears and acting in ways that nurture that opportunity until it bears its fruit. Unfortunately, this is not so easy as you might think, in part because most opportunities arrive unexpectedly, usually as odd coincidences, and disguised in humble attire. For this reason, golden chances are often ignored or dismissed. For those who perceive opportunity when it appears, and know how to nurture it, success is virtually assured. Let me give you another example.

THE MAN IN THE REVOLVING DOOR

For several years, I tried to contact one of the world's wealthiest men to convince him to invest in a company that produces breakthrough medical technologies, including new treatments for infectious and life-threatening diseases. The man I was trying to contact, who will remain anonymous for reasons of privacy, proved unusually difficult to reach. That was disappointing because the company I was representing was led by a remarkable scientist who I believed would revolutionize medicine within the next several years. The problem, of course, was they desperately needed money to do their work.

I was about to give up my efforts at contacting this man when one day I entered a revolving door to an office tower on Park Avenue in New York. Suddenly, the door jammed and trapped me within one of its enclosures. Through the glass, I could see a man in his early 60s, clearly upset, trapped in the enclosure opposite me. I recognized him instantly—he was the man I had been trying to contact these past few years. I pushed hard on the door and felt it start to turn again.

Since he was in the enclosure that led out of the building, and I was in the one that led inside, I had to hurry to catch up with him as he left the building. Once outside, I called him by name. He turned around and assessed me cautiously. I immediately introduced myself and explained that I was a Wall Street investment banker who had been trying to get in touch with him. With that, I handed him my card. We walked a short distance together along Park Avenue, as I explained very briefly what I did. I finished by saying that if I could ever be of service, he should call me.

The next day, his secretary called to invite me to his office, where we talked for more than an hour. Two weeks later, he invested in the company whose scientific work I had hoped he would support.

I was very happy that this man decided to help this group of scientists—in fact, he and three other billionaires funded their work—but the event that made me marvel, as all such events do, was that after years of trying unsuccessfully to contact this man, I unexpectedly encountered him in a revolving door that got stuck at the precise moment that the two of us were held within its circle. What are the odds of that happening? I would like to know. From this improbable event, innumerable lives would be affected, including his and mine, the scientists whose work he would support, and the countless people who would be helped by the medical breakthroughs these scientists would bring about.

THE MYSTERY OF CONNECTION

What brings people together? How is it possible that an ostensibly wrong number from a television producer connects two people who have mutual interests and, later on, mutual needs? What are the odds, I would like to know, that two men should meet in a revolving door and end up participating in a scientific breakthrough that may affect millions of lives?

There are no rational reasons that explain why such improbable events occur in our lives. As I see it, these "coincidences" are evidence of something mysterious and immanent in life that unites us all. They are the outward symptom, a reminder you might say, of the web of life that is constantly connecting people who belong together, and in the process putting opportunities for success and fulfillment in front of us.

These "accidents" are common to all of us. How many times have you met someone, or had a coincidental experience, after which you shook your head and said, "It's a small world"? We have all uttered that sentence at one time or another.

Think back to all the mysterious coincidences that magically arranged your first meeting with the person who would become your spouse. Remember, too, all the little events that had to converge and harmonize for you to get an important job, or meet someone who played a significant role in your life. There is always an element of magic in such opportunities, as if they were orchestrated.

The circumstances that arranged my first meeting with my future wife were strange, but probably no stranger than those surrounding your first encounter with someone important in your life.

After I graduated from college in 1983, I lived abroad for a couple of years. During that time, I periodically looked at my college yearbook. For reasons I never understood, I found myself looking at the yearbook photograph of a particular woman who graduated the same year as I did. Below the picture was the woman's name: Donna Friedman. I don't ever remember seeing her on our campus at the State University of New York at Binghamton. That should not have been surprising, since there were more than 10,000 students at Binghamton. Yet, something about Donna Friedman attracted me. I wondered why we never met.

Three years later, I was standing in Rascals, a New York City nightclub, with several of my friends. At one point, my friend pointed to three attractive women across the dance floor and said to me, "I know one of those girls. Let's go over. I'll introduce you."

As we made our way across the club, I couldn't believe my eyes. One of the women we approached was none other than Donna Friedman. Her face was unmistakable to me. My friend introduced me to one of the other women, who in turn introduced Donna. "You graduated from Binghamton in 1983," I said to her. Obviously taken by surprise, she laughed good-naturedly and said, "How did you know?" I explained that I also went to Binghamton. (I spared her the yearbook story for the moment.) But as we talked, I felt an overwhelming attraction to this woman. It was as if I knew her, but at the same time everything about her was new and exciting. As my friends and I drove home that night, I announced that I had met the woman I was going to marry, which I did on July 3, 1990.

Everyone has stories like this. Our lives have been shaped by unexplainable coincidences and chance meetings. Many of us have been miraculously saved from physical harm simply because we happened to linger a second longer at the corner or were stopped by a friend on the way. Others sat down on a train and found their future spouses or long-lost relatives. I particularly liked the widely reported story of LA police officer Kelly Benitez, who, on September 18, 1998, happened to stop a driver for expired license plates, only to discover that the man driving the car was his long-lost father. The two had been separated since Kelly was four months old. Neither knew that the other was living in Los Angeles. In a wonderful twist of fate,

Kelly Benitez was about to go off duty when he spotted the car with the expired plate. He considered letting another cop deal with the situation, but decided to pursue the matter himself. When Kelly began asking the driver questions, he started to realize who he was, but before Kelly could say a word, the driver, Paul Benitez, said, "Are you Kelly? I'm your dad."

We usually say that such experiences "were meant to be," another sentence that reveals our subtle, if subconscious, awareness of the web of life. We know it's there, and we marvel when we encounter it, but we dismiss any conscious consideration of it. Yet, when you think about it, you realize that most of the important connections we make in life, and certainly those we make in business, have occurred "accidentally," or "coincidentally"—a mutual friend casually introduces you to someone who turns out to be pivotal in your life, or a series of events leads you to a life-altering experience.

Such magical occurrences need not be rare. It is my contention that they are being offered to you on a regular basis. Indeed, if you open up to the opportunities implicit in coincidence, big things are possible. Events can occur that not only affect your life, your family's lives, and the company you work for, but even the course of nations. The following experience illustrates this very point.

WHAT TWO PEOPLE AND COINCIDENCE CAN DO

On a warm evening in the summer of 1991, I hurried out of my hotel room at the Grand Hyatt in Seoul, South Korea, and barely caught the elevator as its doors began to close. Out of habit or restlessness, I pressed the down button for the first floor, which was already illuminated. On the other side of the elevator stood a middle-aged Korean man who looked at me, smiled, and in perfect English asked if I was an American.

"Yes," I said.

"I was curious because very few Americans stay in this hotel," he said. He was a handsome man, dressed in a dark business suit, white shirt, and bright tie.

I explained that I was in Seoul on business and also to attend a conference that was taking place at the Grand Hyatt. The words were no sooner out of my mouth when the man asked me if I would have dinner with him the following night.

"I'm sorry," I said, "but I am leaving for New York tomorrow."

Would it be possible for me to stay another day? he asked. No, I said, because I would be leaving for Israel shortly after getting back to New York.

"Israel?" he said. "I have never been there. Would you mind if I went with you?"

I know what you're thinking, but I sensed this man's sincerity. Something about him suggested that he was more than a lonely businessman who was curious about Americans.

In the hotel lobby, we exchanged business cards. His name was Bruce Lee. (I resisted the obvious jokes.) He was a lawyer who had been educated in the United States, hence his perfect English. He specialized in real estate and international investments, he said. We seemed to have something in common. I told Mr. Lee that I would be traveling to Israel with my wife, but would be happy to have him accompany us. I could introduce him to some of the country's business leaders, if he liked.

We shook hands and parted. I never expected to hear from him again. But two weeks later, Mr. Lee called. He and his wife were in New York and were ready to join us on our trip to Israel.

The day after we arrived in Tel Aviv, the Lees, my wife, Donna, and I met for cocktails at the Sheraton Hotel's restaurant. Mrs. Lee didn't speak English, so Mr. Lee translated the conversation for his wife. At one point, I asked Mr. Lee what his wife did in Korea.

"She coordinates consulate parties in Korea," he replied.

That's an odd job, I thought. Suddenly, an even odder question popped into my mind, but before I could censure myself I asked, "What does her father do?"

"He is President of Korea," Mr. Lee said.

Not believing I heard him correctly, I asked, "President of what company?"

"Not company, *country*," he replied.

The next thing I did was call a friend who set up a meeting with Shalom Zinger, Director General of Finance for the State of Israel. The meeting between Messrs. Lee and Zinger opened up all kinds of possibilities for the two countries. During their discussion, Mr. Lee asked to visit the Korean Embassy in Israel. There is no Korean Embassy, he was informed. Relations between Israel and Korea were superficial, at best. Upon hearing this, Mr. Lee frowned.

Within a year of that meeting, the Korean Embassy was established in Israel and the two countries entered a whole new era in their relationship. Today, Korea is one of Israel's leading per capita trading partners, with trading revenues that have reached well into the billions of dollars. And all of it started from a serendipitous meeting between two men in an elevator on the other side of the world.

* * *

Unfortunately, most people miss opportunities such as this one for the simple reason that such golden chances come to us in unexpected ways and at unexpected moments—a chance telephone call or an improbable meeting in an elevator, for example. What makes our failure to recognize such opportunities even more distressing is that these unexpected moments announce themselves to us as they occur in our lives. It's true that these "announcements" usually come as a whisper, a gentle pull, or a mild but palpable urge to act. The feelings are subtle, to be sure, but they are there. Unfortunately, most of us ignore the call. It's as if we shrink in the presence of a gift.

WHY WE REFUSE THE GIFT

Of course, one of the primary reasons we refuse the gift is because of fear. We think that if we act we will be hurt in some way or disappointed because we will fail. Fear closes us to the possibilities; it shrinks our imagination and prevents us from seeing the good in the person or the potential in the event. Fear arises because, as we venture into the unknown, we believe that bad things will happen. In fact, we don't know what might happen, but we assume that it may be bad, so we resist.

Albert Einstein said that every one of us must ask and answer one single question in life. That question is this: "Is the universe a friendly place?" As Einstein said, our answer to that question determines both our character and the quality of our lives. It also determines whether we see coincidence as danger or opportunity.

For those who say "yes, the universe is essentially a friendly place—at least to me," life is rich with possibilities, largely because these people are able to act positively and proactively when "coincidental" opportunity presents itself.

Take, for example, the experience of my good friend, actress Fran Drescher, who found herself sitting on the same flight as Jeff Sagansky, the president of CBS Networks six years ago. At the time, Fran had done small parts in some good films, including *Saturday Night Fever*, but had not yet achieved the success she was about to experience. Fran had what she believed to be a great idea for a weekly situation comedy that she titled "The Nanny." She knew she could make such a show work, if only she could pitch it to the right person. And now, by some strange coincidence, she found herself sitting in the same first-class cabin as Jeff Sagansky, the very man who could make her idea become a reality. This was her moment and she knew it. Fran got up from her seat, went to the bathroom, looked at herself in the mirror, and repeated the words *carpe diem* several times. On her way back to her seat, she "happened" to notice Mr. Sagansky. "What a surprise! I'm Fran Drescher."

For six years, "The Nanny" was a ratings-winner and one of CBS's strongest shows. It is shown in syndication around the world.

Fran's courage was possible because, first, she recognized the opportunity implicit in the coincidence of Mr. Sagansky's presence; second, she believed that, if she pitched her show, Jeff Sagansky would give her a fair hearing; and third, she believed in herself enough to make a good, even great, impression. In essence, she trusted in the essential friendliness of the circumstances, which made it possible to take the risk. As her experience proved, her beliefs were all true, which is why her dream became reality.

Making the web of life work for you depends on your openness to the possibilities within coincidence. Don't get me wrong. I'm not suggesting that you suspend good judgment or jump willy-nilly into situations that seem threatening. On the contrary, listen to your gut in all cases. When coincidences-bearing-gifts arrive, they excite and awaken you to the possibilities at hand. At that moment, it is only fear that holds you back, and only fear that limits your potential for growth and success. Know that when coincidence and inspiration strike, the chances are good that you may very well be looking at the beginning of a long chain of events that will lead you to success. Just as it did for Tom Stemberg.

Tom Stemberg had a long career as senior manager in supermarkets and eventually became president of Edwards-Finast. One day he was fired from his job. While he was still unemployed, Tom found himself shopping in a Massachusettes department store. There he noticed that the products in the office supply section were strewn about chaotically on the shelves. There is a lot of activity here, Tom thought to himself. This must be a popular line of products. But look what a mess it is. The store managers don't maintain it, which means they don't realize how important these products really are. Suddenly, lightning struck. Why not start a store that specialized only in office supplies? Inspired by his great idea, Tom managed to raise the capital he needed to start Staples, which today does more than $5 billion in annual sales.

Perhaps if Tom showed up at that store on any other day, the items on those shelves would have been perfectly arranged, or perhaps he would not have had the clarity to perceive the underlying message implicit on those messy shelves. But the events came together—as did the financing—and Staples was born.

WHEN THE COINCIDENCE ARRIVES, LOOK FOR THE OPPORTUNITY

Life becomes larger, richer, and more exciting when you open up to greater possibilities for yourself, your family, and all the people you care about. At the same time, you will also experience more of your own power, because you will see how you can be guided by your own abilities and intuition. Today, when my gut tells me to pursue something, I try to listen. Not every endeavor succeeds, of course. As I said, I have failed as many times as I have succeeded, but I'll take a .500 batting average any day. I have learned that my inner voice can provide very good counsel, indeed.

In 1997, Michael P. Schulof, the former president and CEO of Sony Entertainment, took the offices next to mine. On the second day in his new office, I introduced myself and told his secretary that I would be happy to help her settle in to the new building. (Sometimes I can be slightly audacious.)

Later in the year, I was introduced to a new technology that utilized particle physics in animation. Apparently, the new physics gave the animation a three-dimensional quality and made the process of creating animated films much faster. It sounded very interesting to me, but because I am neither a physicist nor an animator, I did not fully understand the technology, nor all of its implications. On a hunch, I decided to mention the new technology to Mr. Schulof and asked if he would be interested in talking to the inventor, who lived in Paris. He politely declined my offer. Oddly, my gut told me that he might be interested if he got the right presentation, so I sent him the related materials anyway. (Sometimes I can be *more* than slightly audacious.)

Three weeks later, I telephoned Mr. Schulof again and told him that the inventor and company CEO, Dr. Eyal Cohen, was in New York. Would he like to meet him? This time, Mr. Schulof said yes. He very much wanted to meet Mr. Cohen.

What followed was a series of meetings, two of which took place in Paris, and three months of negotiations, after which Mr. Schulof emerged as the chairman of Animation Science. As it turned out, Mr. Schulof has a Ph.D. in physics, a little coincidence that I did not know when I sent him the materials that described the new company. When I learned that he was a physicist, I could only shake my head and wonder at what unknown hand had pointed me in his direction. And to put a cherry on top of the whole affair, I later learned that Mr. Schulof and Mr. Cohen were married to women who were distant cousins from Greece. It wasn't until after the two families became business partners that anyone knew of their close family ties.

FROM HUMBLE COINCIDENCE
CAN COME GREATNESS

I believe that if you look back at the careers of great people, you will find some pivotal moment that changed the direction of their lives and indeed put them on the course toward prodigious achievement. If you look closer, you will find that, very often, that pivotal moment was a seemingly mundane event, a mere coincidence, that changed everything. Take for instance the experience of David Sarnoff, the man who made RCA into the corporate giant we know today.

In 1906, a 15-year-old boy by the name of David Sarnoff decided that he wanted a job as a reporter at the *New York Herald*. Sarnoff had no skills, little education, and apparently a poor sense of direction because on the day he went for his interview at the *Herald,* he accidentally wandered into the business offices of the Commercial Cable Company, a telegraph firm located in the same building as the newspaper. "I'm looking for a job on the newspaper," he told the cable company's office manager.

"I don't know about the *Herald,*" the office manager told him, "but we can use another messenger boy in our shop."

At that moment, Sarnoff had a decision to make. He could have politely declined and eventually found the *Herald's* offices. Instead, he took the job. Once there, Sarnoff studied the telegraph industry and fell in love with the possibilities offered by wireless communication. He had stumbled into a whole new form of communication that was just beginning to link distant places and far away peoples.

A few months later, Commercial Cable fired him because he wanted to take time off for the Jewish high holy days, but by that time Sarnoff had already found his niche in life and was immediately hired by the Marconi Wireless Telegraph Company. There he began his long ascent from office boy to president of the company that later would be renamed the Radio Corporation of America, or RCA. Under Sarnoff, RCA would pioneer the development of radio, television, and broadcast entertainment. And it all began when, as a young boy, he made a "mistake" by entering the "wrong" office.

THE WEB NEVER FORGETS

The web of life seems to have a long memory and an even longer reach, returning to each of us good fortune or bad, depending on the seeds we have sown. The good you do is never forgotten, I believe. In fact, I have seen the evidence to support that belief turn up from time to time, very often when I needed it most.

When I was a year old, my parents owned a two-family house in Brooklyn and rented the downstairs apartment to the Francos, a family of Cuban refugees. They were a husband, a wife, and a five-year-old boy. Mrs. Franco didn't speak a word of English. At night, the boy, whose name was Izzy, would come up to our apartment and get help with his homework from my mother. As I got older, I would watch my mother as she helped my older brother with his homework, and then start again with Izzy. After about five years, the family moved away and we never saw or heard from them again. I didn't remember much about Izzy except that he loved to build the most intricate model ships. He had tremendous dexterity with his hands and could labor over those ships for hours, putting every little piece perfectly in place.

Thirty years passed. Donna and I married and had three children. Recently, we discovered that our oldest child needed surgery. Naturally, we were concerned, though the operation was supposed to be fairly routine. In a discussion with my wife, our family pediatrician recommended a pediatric surgeon at Westchester Medical Center. The doctor's name was Israel Franco. My wife called the doctor and made an appointment to meet him to discuss our son's condition. After they arrived, my wife introduced herself and my son to the doctor, who responded that he once knew a family by the name of Kash. "I grew up with a family that had three sons—Peter, Eric, and Douglas," the doctor said. "I think they spelled their name with a C, though."

Amazed, Donna said, "No, they spell their name with a K and Peter is my husband."

Suddenly, Dr. Franco's face turned into a big smile. "I owe my medical degree to Mrs. Kash. She helped me with my English and got me through my first few years of school in America."

This man, who as a boy studied at our dining room table with my mother, was now the surgeon who operated on our son. All went well and my son made a rapid and wonderful recovery. Of course, my gratitude was so great that I was moved to tears. But I will never forget the look on Izzy's face when he came out of that operating room, took my hands in his, and said, "Your son is fine. Everything went well." It was as if both of us had come full circle and had fulfilled an important debt of gratitude to one another.

My experience reminds me of that far more famous account in which a Scottish farmer by the name of Fleming saved the life of the young Winston Churchill, who, when he was just a boy, got stuck in a bog and was about to drown. When Churchill's father found out what had happened to his son, he went back to the farmer and offered him a reward. The farmer refused the offer. Just then, his son ran out of their house. The senior Churchill saw the boy and offered to give him a good education. The farmer thought about it for a few seconds and agreed. The boy eventually went to St. Mary's Hospital Medical School in London and went on to be knighted as Sir Alexander Fleming, the discoverer of penicillin. Of course, the young Churchill made good as well, becoming one of England's greatest prime ministers. Interestingly, the two would cross paths once more. At one point in his esteemed career, Churchill became severely ill with pneumonia; his life was saved when he was given penicillin.

As I will illustrate in the chapters that follow, life is constantly reminding us that the good we do—or the bad, for that matter—somehow finds its way back to us, again and again. As the biblical aphorism says, plant good seeds and many rewards will follow. Essentially that means to treat people in ways that recognize their dignity and inherent goodness and to promote their lives whenever possible. In other words, make a lot of friends along the way. This seems pretty basic, but unfortunately all too many people see this approach as antithetical in our competitive world. As I will show, the businesspeople who maintain this ethic are usually the ones who go the farthest in their careers—and sleep the deepest at night.

A WINK FROM THE WEB OF LIFE

Very often, we are reminded of the interconnectedness of life by small events and strange coincidences that do not change our lives, but instead just amuse or amaze us. It's as if the web of life were winking at us, reminding us of its underlying presence, but not intruding too much on the normal order of things. Very often, we are a lot closer to our greatest dreams, as well as our little fantasies, than the standard six-degrees-of-separation might suggest.

When I was just a teenager, I had a crush on actress Brooke Shields. I remember telling my girlfriend at the time that if I ever got the chance to have a date with Brooke Shields, I would leap at the opportunity. "Don't worry," my girlfriend said, "you'll never meet Brook Shields."

In 1991, a Japanese friend and business partner asked me if I could arrange to have Brooke Shields do a photography session with Hiromi Go, roughly the Japanese equivalent of our own Billy Joel. "Why not," I said. From my office, I yelled out to our executive assistant, Donna Lozito: "How can I find Brooke Shields?" She smiled, got up from her desk, and entered my office. "I used to babysit for Brooke when she was just a little kid," she said. That was all the help I needed. A month later, Brooke and her mother, who helped manage her daughter's career, had agreed to do the shoot at New York's Plaza Hotel. Before the session, I picked up Brooke at her home. She greeted me at her front door with a little kiss on the cheek and later that night, after the photography session was over, I took her out to dinner. One of the amazing things about Brooke Shields was that during our meal she was interrupted by perhaps a dozen people who wanted her autograph. She had a smile and a kind remark for every one of them.

After I had my "date" with Brooke Shields, I called my old girlfriend, who is still a friend, and told her of my wonderful evening with my long-time fantasy. "Only you, Peter. Only you," was her reply. That's where she was wrong.

MAKING THE WEB WORK FOR YOU

Tremendous opportunities occur when we connect with people in a positive way. Very often, coincidence is opportunity knocking. In order to make the most of these golden chances, we must first understand that something good often lies in events that seem humble and even meaningless, at least on the surface.

Our value system helps us to make the most of our opportunities. These two are the yin and yang of the web of life, you might say. Together, the two ensure that success and personal enrichment combine to make us more humane. In the following chapter, I'm going to show you how opportunity and values are intimately intertwined, and how your success depends on both.

CHAPTER 2

The Secret Basis
for Success
and Fulfillment

First ask yourself: What is the worst that can happen?
Then prepare to accept it. Then proceed to
improve on the worst.

—Dale Carnegie

*O*ne of the axioms I tell my students is this: One thing, more than any other, will determine how your life turns out. That thing is neither money nor fame. Rich and famous people wind up miserable and ruined every day of the week. The thing that will determine whether you are loved, respected, successful, and fulfilled will be your values—not the values you think you have, or the ones you would like to have, but those that you live every day.

One of the primary places where your values will be revealed will be in business. Contrary to what is widely presented in the media and taught today at colleges, business is done cooperatively. And it is done best in an atmosphere of trust. Behaviors that promote distrust only serve to pollute the atmosphere and prevent optimal working conditions. They cause companies to lose opportunities and money; consequently, they often get people fired or land a company in court. Yet, it is very difficult for people at all levels of their careers—especially those just starting out—to realize that the characteristics that promote trust also form the foundation for successful careers and fulfilled lives.

I have worked with and known people at virtually every level of the social ladder and had a chance to study the characteristics that lead to success and personal fulfillment. Many of the people I work with are high-income earners, some of whom appear on *Forbes's* annual list of wealthiest Americans. I have also worked with people who would not be considered financially wealthy, but are fulfilled in their work and rich in many other areas of their lives. Those who are personally fulfilled, even happy, no matter what their status may be, have achieved such success because they maintain certain simple human values—honesty, integrity, courage, and straightforwardness—that form the foundation for a successful and rewarding life. It isn't that they don't make mistakes or haven't failed. On the contrary, every one of the most fulfilled people I know have made many mistakes and failed numerous times. Despite their setbacks, however, they continued to strive toward their goals and what they believed in.

Interestingly, true fulfillment—that is, a deep satisfaction with who you are and what you have become—is only conferred if you develop your humanity as you pursue your goals. Yes, great wealth is often achieved by people who are arrogant, selfish, and even mean. But my experience has shown that these people are also miserable. It's as if they got one of their goals, wealth, but violated a whole set of human principles and, in the process, became distorted, wretched, and deeply unhappy.

There is a very simple reason for this fundamental truth about life, which is this: Of all there is to say about values, one of the most fundamental is that the values that lead to a successful life are already woven into the very fibers of your being.

They are as natural to you as your own heart. The problem is that most of us don't know it. Through experience, courage, and effort, we come to know these values. At that point, it is our job to live them. If you spend your life violating these principles, you will end up judging yourself very harshly, and even shrinking in your own eyes. I dare say you may end up even hating yourself. The reason is that in the end, each of us is our own worst and toughest judge. We make our judgment by evaluating our lives according to a set of values that is already inside of us.

Allow me to recount a story a friend of mine told me recently as a way to illustrate this point.

One day while traveling, my friend happened to look out the window of his hotel room and saw—two stories below—two young boys, perhaps eight or nine years of age, walking down the street directly opposite his room, both apparently enjoying the bright, sunny day. Suddenly, one of the boys stuck his right leg in front of his friend's legs and twisted his body so that his leg clamped his friend's legs together, causing the second boy to come crashing down onto the sidewalk, face first. Even though his hotel windows were sealed, my friend said he could feel the impact of the boy's face smashing into the pavement. The boy's nose was instantly bloodied and his right cheek scratched. He rolled around on the sidewalk and cried out in pain.

The boy who tripped him looked around to see if anyone had witnessed what he had done. Satisfied that the coast was clear, he attempted to help his friend up, but the boy who had fallen refused to rise. He made a feeble attempt at swatting his friend's hand away and went on crying. Soon a couple of adults appeared; one applied a handkerchief to the boy's nose and turned his head back to stop the bleeding. Another helped him get up.

Just as this was happening, a third young boy appeared on the scene. He observed the events with disinterest and started conversing with the culprit. A few minutes later, these two boys left. As they walked away, the perpetrator of the event showed the new boy how his friend had tripped over his own two feet. In slow motion, the perpetrator mimed again and again how his friend got his feet tangled up together, and how this innocent mistake had caused him to come crashing down on the ground. As he demonstrated for his friend how the "accident" had happened, he gestured with his hand to show how the pavement had come up and smashed his friend in the face and bloodied his nose.

Obviously, he was creating an alternate story for what had really taken place, my friend pointed out. The boy was working hard to convince himself that he was innocent, though his companion seemed even more indifferent to the explanation than he was to the event. Still, despite his companion's apathy, the culprit went on explaining the matter with great animation and apparently in considerable detail, showing several times how the boy's feet got tangled up together and brought about his fall. It was almost as if his explanation was a wish that the events had happened as he was saying they did.

"Not only did he hurt the kid," my friend told me, "but he went down the street lying about it to another kid. Can you believe it?"

Yes, I thought. Not only do I believe it, but I know how the young perpetrator felt. The reason the young boy was actively denying the truth, I realized, was because he was having trouble accepting his own actions.

The question is: Why do we have so much trouble accepting our actions that we know to be harmful to others? Why do we feel compelled to lie about the things we do that are wrong?

I considered this little puzzle on and off for the rest of the day and thought about it for many days afterward. Even as an adult, I have made mistakes that I later had trouble accepting. Whenever I have been rude to someone, or offered information that was less than full disclosure, I suffered pangs of conscience that very often forced me to go back and either apologize or explain matters more fully.

I have spoken to others about these kinds of experiences and have heard people report similar struggles. After much consideration, I am now convinced that some basic ethics are fundamental to human nature. They even may be woven into our DNA. After millions of years of evolution—which is to say, millions of years of living together in small communities—something deep inside of us now demands that we act ethically toward one another. It isn't just our modern social education that informs you not to lie, steal, or kill; it's our nature not to do these things. Every time our behavior is in harmony with these values, we experience a psychological reward that can only be described as a kind of spiritual high. Allow me to give you an example.

When I was a young teenager, I used to work as a camp counselor at the Raleigh Hotel in the Catskills. One of the managers of the hotel was a man in his mid-50s named Mace Teicher. Firm and lovable, Mace radiated ethics and character. The children called him "Uncle Macc." One winter, I managed to get my best friend, Gary Stein, a job as a counselor at the Raleigh Hotel. On the night before he was to arrive at the hotel to start his job, Gary was driving through his hometown of Bellmore, Long Island, when his car skidded on the icy street and slammed into a parked Cadillac, denting the fender. It was about midnight when the accident occurred and the street was very dark. Gary got out of his car and went up to the house in front of which the Cadillac was parked. He rang the doorbell and a man came to the door. Gary asked if the Cadillac was his.

"Yes," the man said.

"I'm very sorry," said Gary, "but I just hit your car. Here's my driver's license and insurance information."

The man was surprised, especially since he hadn't heard a thing. He looked at Gary carefully, took down the information, and thanked him for his honesty.

The next day, Gary arrived at the Raleigh and, just in passing, told me of the incident. At one point late in the afternoon, we brought our kids to the dining room, where we unexpectedly encountered Mace Teicher. Gary had never met Mace before, so I said, "Come over here. I want to introduce you to Mace."

As I made the introductions, Gary and Mace stood smiling at one another, as if they knew each other. Gary turned to me and said, "This is the man whose car I hit last night." Mace's grin grew even larger and so did Gary's. I noticed that the two looked at each other with mutual respect and appreciation. Something fundamentally good and human had connected them now and they knew it.

"So this is the kind of person you have us hire, eh Kash?" With that, Mace slapped both of us on the backs and walked away.

There was no other reward from that incident, nor was another needed. I felt the glow of that encounter and was reminded of what Plato says in the *Republic:* Doing good is its own reward. There are moments in your life when nothing can touch the feeling of having done something honest and good—and for no other reason than it was right.

This must surely have been what Esther Kim, a 20-year-old tae kwon do practitioner, experienced when she gave her place on the U.S. Olympic team to her dear friend and competitor, Kay Poe. Tae kwon do was a medal event in the 2000 Summer games. Kim and Poe had known each other for 13 years and, as Kim said, the two were like sisters. Both were competing for the flyweight spot on the team and both had made the final round of the elimination tournament that would decide who went to Sydney, Australia for the 2000 games. Poe had beaten Kim the last time they competed and was the favorite for the gold medal at the Olympic games. But in her previous bout, Poe had had her kneecap dislocated and would have to fight Kim essentially on one leg. Under such conditions, Kim would likely have been the winner and thus would have gone to Sydney to represent the U.S. Instead, Kim decided to forfeit to Poe and give her place on the team to her friend. Before the match, the two talked about the unfair conditions the two would be facing.

"We have to fight," Poe said. "I'll do the best I can." Said Kim: "You can't even stand up. How are you going to fight?"

When Kim told Poe that she planned to forfeit the match, Poe insisted that such a thing would be wrong, but Kim had already decided. "I wouldn't be losing my dream, I'd be handing it to Kay," Kim told *The New York Times* on May 25, 2000. "I couldn't live with myself knowing I beat someone who had already been beaten."

When the two went to the mat to compete, both were crying. Kim forfeited and Poe was announced the winner.

"It felt like the only right thing to do," Kim said later. "It did hurt, but winning a gold medal isn't everything. There are other ways to be a champion. If I don't have a gold medal around my neck, it's in my heart."

Somehow, we know that Esther Kim is a champion and that she will be fine, gold medal or not. Her act has brought worldwide attention to her, and deservedly so. In addition to being written about in *The New York Times,* she was also featured in major magazines. The reason she has gained so much attention is because she awakens us all to the fact that there is a higher goal than winning—that doing right is of greater importance than doing well. Esther Kim's act of heroism resonates inside of us. It plucks the strings on our own inherent values, and reminds us that something inside each of us is striving to do good.

WHEN YOU BREAK YOUR PRINCIPLES, OWN IT

It's as natural to break our values as it is to have them, which explains why so many people hurt others and get themselves into trouble. It's also true that after making such mistakes, the vast majority of us suffer some kind of internal disharmony, a symptom of which is emotional or psychological pain. Depending on how great the ethical mistake, that pain can throw us into crisis.

The worst thing we can do when we make such a mistake, however, is to deny it or run away from it. Running away from pain causes a whole array of other problems, not the least of which is more pain.

I remember a time several years ago when I had a man from New Jersey who was a potential investor in my office. He was considering investing in a new company I was helping to start up. During our meeting, I accepted five or six telephone calls. When the meeting ended, we parted cordially, but afterwards my acceptance of those calls weighed heavily on my conscience. I had been rude to this man and we both knew it. He didn't like what I had done and, the more I thought about it, neither did I. Needless to say, he never invested with me.

Three years later, I was invited to Brazil to meet a group of investors. This would be my first trip to Brazil and I asked my secretary to find out if I needed a special visa to enter the country. No, she told me, no special visa was needed in Brazil. When I arrived, Brazilian customs barred me from entering because I did not have an entry visa. I was quickly deported to Buenos Aires, Argentina, where I stayed in a hotel and tried to obtain a visa to enter Brazil from the American consulate there. While in Buenos Aires, I went out to dinner and as the web of life would have it I bumped into the prospective investor from New Jersey whom I had met in my office three years before. Now in the restaurant, he was with his wife and another couple. They all were about to leave the restaurant. Amazed at seeing him so far away from home, I went over to him as he was about to leave the restaurant to say hello. He looked at me and said, "You can't be serious." He turned and walked away. I knew instantly the reason for his snub.

Naturally, I felt embarrassed and hurt. It would have been easy for me to become preoccupied with this man's rudeness, which at the time seemed greater than my own. But if I had done that, I would have missed the important lesson that this man had now taught me twice—once in New York and now again in Buenos Aires: Never treat people with anything less than respect. I had treated him badly and now he was doing the same to me. What I did was ethically wrong and bad for business. The truth is, the two usually go hand-in-hand.

Yet, if someone had asked me before I met this New Jersey businessman if respect for others was an important ethic for me, I would have said, "Absolutely. I just screwed up." But that ethic hadn't been so deeply learned as I had thought. I'll bet that that little boy who tripped his friend knew better than to do what he did, too, but that didn't stop him from doing it. Sometimes you've got to learn the hard way by making mistakes. Sometimes you've got to go back five steps in order to go forward twenty.

My experience with my New Jersey acquaintance made me realize that I, like most other people, have an implicit ethical code within me that I must accept and live out if I have any chance of being the person I want to be in life. My challenge, in a sense, is to *remember* my own inner code and act accordingly. This is the case for most people, I believe. Not only do we have an implicit ethical code inside of us, but that code is very similar for most of us.

Yes, there is a minority of people out there who, either by genetic mutation or failure of their education, have no inner code. They have to live with that and its consequences. Fortunately, these people are a very tiny minority in the grand scheme of things. The world is held together and maintained by the rest of us who are struggling with our ethics and values and who acknowledge that such a struggle involves making mistakes, suffering the pain of self-examination, and learning from those mistakes. The people who are engaged, to varying degrees, in some version of this process make up the majority of the people on Earth, I believe. In other words, most people are inherently good and, even more important, they are trying to do the right thing.

My belief that the world is made up of essentially good people is based on my experience in business and in life. I have traveled to and done business in more than 50 countries on six continents and I can tell you that no matter what the nationality or the religious or ethnic background of the people I have met, the overwhelming majority have been good people who wanted to believe that I was a person of sound values, like themselves. This realization is one reason why I answer Einstein's famous question—Is the universe a friendly place?—in the affirmative.

Interestingly, there are those very wise people who do not answer Einstein's question with either a yes or a no, but rather say that the universe is what you make it. In other words, each of us creates the character of our own world. The man who taught me this was one of the most noble people I have ever met.

MAKING THE UNIVERSE
A FRIENDLY PLACE FOR YOU

I do a lot of business in Asia. Consequently, I have had the good fortune to spend considerable time there and have come to know some of its best business leaders. Many people in Asia believe that the universe isn't arbitrarily friendly or unfriendly. Rather, the nature of the universe depends on your behavior. Wise people attempt to make the universe friendly by cultivating good karma. One day, I was walking down Seventh Avenue in New York with my friend and business associate, Tamio Nishizawa, president of Yamaichi Univen America, the venture capital division of Yamaichi Bank, which at the time was the fourth largest bank in the world. Despite his success, Mr. Nishizawa is a man of great humility, which, paradoxically, radiates from him as tremendous dignity. As we walked briskly down Seventh Avenue together, we encountered more than a dozen men and women who stood outside of restaurants and store fronts handing out menus and advertisements for their businesses. Most people simply ignore these street hawkers, but Mr. Nishizawa accepted every single menu and advertisement that was offered to him. Finally, after his hands were full of these things, I turned to Mr. Nishizawa and said, "Nishizawa-san, why do you accept every one of these menus and ads from these people? Do you intend to go to these restaurants and stores?"

"If I can support them in doing their job, perhaps people will support me in doing my job," was his response. With those words, he instantly gave me a picture of the web of life—a vast interwoven fabric that gives us back exactly what we give out. In that moment, I was this man's student. He was teaching me something basic and profound about how we should treat people in all walks of life.

Karma is essentially the philosophy of cause and effect. Every one of your actions is a cause that creates an effect. Good causes result in good effects. Good seeds beget good fruit. Mr. Nishizawa was saying, in essence, that the universe is good to those who make good causes.

Karma is just another way of saying "what goes around comes around," or, more simply, the web of life. Sometimes the web responds quickly to our planting of good seeds, and sometimes it is slow; but eventually it responds, especially if we have maintained our courage, perseverance, and right actions. I am not saying for a second that bad things don't happen to good people. In fact, bad things happen to all of us, good and bad, but far more good accrues to those who consistently do good, than it does to those who act poorly toward others. Certainly, all of us know this in our hearts.

We know that honesty, courage, integrity, and straightforwardness are the foundations for character, honor, and order in the world. No one has to be told such a thing. What we need, I believe, is the encouragement to make such virtues part of our lives. That can only happen through continual effort and the willingness to learn from our mistakes. If the aforementioned values are the foundation for success, the principles I name below are the walls, rooms, and roof of the great edifice you can make of your career and your life. Here are just a few that, I believe, are the secrets to success.

HAVE INTEGRITY, BUT FIRST UNDERSTAND WHAT IT IS

Most of us believe that integrity means doing what you say you will do. That's correct, as far as it goes. Unfortunately, that definition can and often does cause good people to suffer tremendous misery and even the loss of their integrity. The reason: We often say yes to the wrong things, or we say yes when we really mean no. Then our integrity is compromised and we appear weak, or ineffective, or unworthy of trust. No one wants to be seen that way.

Therefore, rather than go on about how important integrity is, I want to address a deeper issue that in fact determines whether you have integrity or not. That deeper issue is this: understanding what you are committing to, before you commit, and why you are making such a commitment. Having integrity should not be all that difficult, if you understand yourself and take a realistic look at the challenges to which you commit yourself.

The first thing we must understand about integrity is that it's essentially a self-centered virtue. By self-centered, I mean that one speaks and acts from the core of his or her being. All too often, people commit to doing something because they think it's what someone else wants them to do. In a sense, we say we will do something to make someone else happy. Sometimes we believe that by making someone else happy, we'll make ourselves happy. Unfortunately, that kind of thinking often backfires.

How many of us have taken a job or an assignment from our employer, knowing full well that we were not committed to that job or project? In fact, we knew that we didn't really want to do what we were being asked to do. The simple answer is, all of us. At one time or another, we have all found ourselves in that situation. Okay, fine. But if you find yourself doing this over and over again, you are in the wrong profession. Even worse, you are out of integrity with your soul. You cannot possibly succeed in such a profession, because you will naturally hold back your full commitment from the job.

If you're lucky, you'll get fired or laid off. But if you somehow manage to remain in that position for a long time, you will lose something more important than your job—you'll lose all contact with your soul. Gradually, you'll find yourself shrinking from the job, and then from life itself, until you lose your dreams and become the person I described earlier—the man or woman who is dying of cynicism.

Before you commit yourself to an important endeavor, ask yourself whether or not you *can* do the thing that you are being asked to do. You may not be able to do it. Maybe you don't have the time; maybe you have other commitments; perhaps your expertise is in another area. In most cases, there's absolutely nothing wrong with saying you simply are unable to do it.

Being *able* to do something is only the first step, however. Second, ask yourself if you really *want* to do it. Are you *willing*? Can you commit yourself fully to this endeavor, or will you naturally hold yourself back from it, in part because you inherently don't want to do it? Also ask yourself what your motivations are. What are the benefits to you? Is the goal worth achieving? Is it worth the effort you will have to put forth in order to accomplish your goal? The goal may be so exciting that you feel it's worth the effort you will have to make. Finally, ask yourself if you are doing this thing from your own heart or if you are doing it because you want to make someone else happy at your own expense.

Very often, people make the mistake, especially early in their careers, of habitually telling people what they want to hear. They do this without searching themselves for what they really feel inside about a particular task or challenge.

"What choice do I have?" many people ask at this point. "I have to do what my boss asks me to do."

The truth is, everyone has a choice. You can either give yourself entirely to the challenge you are facing, or you can retreat from it and give the minimum effort. People who choose the latter course are silently and perhaps subconsciously saying to themselves and their employer that they don't want to do the job they are being asked to do, and in fact are refusing to give themselves entirely to the task at hand. This is a dangerous practice for two reasons. First, it can eventually get you fired. Second and even more dangerous, it may become a habit that you never break out of. That can be disastrous, not only for your career—you'll never amount to very much by doing the minimum—but also for your life.

What working hard has taught me is that most challenges that offer a worthwhile goal, or benefit, are actually harder to achieve than they appear to be at first. Once you commit yourself to an endeavor, you will encounter unexpected difficulties, trials, and struggles that you never anticipated. They are part of the package. Very few things that are worth achieving are easy. This means that your commitment will be challenged. If you only make a half-hearted commitment at the outset, your chances of failing are better than 50 percent. Therefore, the more you commit to things that you are essentially unwilling to do, the more failure you will experience in your life. It's that simple.

SECOND, BELIEVE IN WHAT YOU ARE DOING

One of the things that some people believe upon entering their business careers is that they can do their jobs just for the money. The truth is, most of us have to believe in what we do in order to do it well. Something in the human spirit demands that we find meaning in our lives and in our work. I don't care what you do, whether you make shoes or tennis racquets—the world needs both—it is imperative that you recognize the essential goodness of your work and its contribution to society. For a time, especially early in our careers, we can deny the importance of such a belief. We can even work for people or an industry that is having a negative effect on society or the world. But eventually, it catches up to most of us. And when it does, it makes a wreck of our lives.

Believing in your work, knowing that you are making a difference in the world, allows you to throw yourself entirely into your career. When you do that, the web of life will provide you with opportunities in places where you least expect them.

A few years ago, I was in a hospital delivery room with my beautiful wife, Donna, who was about to give birth. The delivery was going slowly. During the sixteen hours of labor, Donna's doctor and I got to talking about the future of medicine, especially as it related to his own field of obstetrics.

It just so happened that I was looking for investors in a company whose technology could revolutionize pediatric science. The more I spoke about this technology, the more interested our doctor became. At one point our conversation became very involved and Donna began to wonder whether the doctor was paying more attention to me than he was to her. Of course, he was more focused on her than me, but she was the one suffering and she needed all the attention she could get from him. Eventually, Donna gave birth to Colby, a beautiful, vivacious baby boy. And three weeks later, I had a new friend and investor. Still, to this day my wife likes to chide me that while she was crying out for an epidural, I was distracting her physician with the finer points of a new and exciting technology. She still doesn't let me live this down.

NOT ME, BUT WE

One of the principles that the Japanese cultivate is the recognition that success is achieved through cooperation and joint efforts, rather than the work of any single individual. The Japanese symbol for people is shaped like a tepee, with two lines converging at the apex. If either line is removed, the other line falls. The image symbolizes our interdependence with each other for survival and success. This is especially true in business. Business works best—that is, more people experience success and personal fulfillment—when we maintain certain values that are mutually supportive.

This same principle prevails at many successful companies in the U.S., as well. At Microsoft, for example, there are more than 30,000 millionaires, many of them secretaries. The reason: Microsoft made stock available to its employees. Those who purchased that stock when the company was still in its infancy are now wealthy beyond their wildest dreams.

The same phenomenon occurred at Home Depot, where workers who bought stock also became wealthy. In fact, many of the floor workers and drivers at Home Depot who later became wealthy continued to hold on to their jobs.

I have instituted the same policy at my own company. Everyone who works with me has shares in every deal I make, for the simple reason that I can do very little without the help of those around me. Therefore, the financial rewards match the reality: We will all succeed together, or we will fail together.

When we are all in the same boat and each of us has something personal at stake, we have a great incentive to work cooperatively. But more than that, by sharing the wealth we acknowledge the integral role people have in the creation of any success. This has a profound impact on those who work with us. It promotes loyalty. People know they are appreciated.

Being appreciated is one of the things people want most in their jobs. They want to know that they count. Unfortunately, it's very common for people to feel unappreciated by their employers. That's a big problem in America today. But when people find a job where they feel they are respected and appreciated, they will put their hearts into their work. And that is one of the most important keys to success.

A common cliché these days is that it takes a village to raise a child. In fact, it takes a team to accomplish virtually anything of value in business. We must all become team players. With the right team of people, we can accomplish almost anything—and what makes it even better is that we can really enjoy ourselves while we do it.

PEOPLE DO BUSINESS—
BUSINESS DOES NOT DO PEOPLE

Opportunities are offered by people. They don't come spitting out of computers or copying machines. If you treat people with respect and dignity, the opportunities that people can provide will flow to you naturally. Just by recognizing that people are more than the titles on their business cards, and then behaving in a way that is consistent with that knowledge, makes you a much more appealing person to do business with. Here are just two examples of how this principle led to important successes in my own life.

In 1989, I lived on 57th Street on the east side of Manhattan. One day I looked out my window and happened to notice that one of the stores below my apartment was flying the Spanish flag. Suddenly, a mysterious urge came over me to do business in Spain. I telephoned the embassy and asked how I could contact potential investors living in Spain who were interested in biotechnology. The person at the embassy transferred my call to the commercial attaché, who gave me a list of people with whom I could correspond. Within a couple of weeks, I was in Madrid, at the Banco Inversion, where I met Pepe Diaz, a senior executive who would become not only an important client, but a friend and business associate. I spent several days getting to know Pepe, not only in his role at the bank, but as a person. I also got to know his bank better—the kinds of people who led the bank, the customers they served, and the ambitions the bank's leadership had for their company. I then presented Pepe with several possible investment opportunities and told him to take whatever time he needed to decide. With that, I returned home.

Two things happened when I got back to my office the following week that surprised me. The first was that another associate of mine informed me that he had also attempted to do business with Pepe and Banco Inversion, without success. The second was that a few days later Pepe called to tell me that he and the bank were investing with me.

"Why?" I asked when he called to give me the news. "I was just told by one of my partners that you had already been approached by our company and that you would not do business with us."

"Unlike your associate, you did not ask us to fill out an account form upon meeting us. You wanted to know us, our bank, and our future needs. That made the difference for us."

Over the next few years, Pepe Diaz would go on to become one of the most successful fund managers in all of Europe and would later be made president and CEO of Banco Inversion. Clearly, Pepe was a client worth getting to know.

Treat Those Below You With Dignity and Respect

It's natural to treat accomplished people with respect and dignity. Very often these people have power and position; therefore, it's easy to hold them in high regard. But one of the things that will reveal your character and values is how you treat people who are below you on the company totem pole, or those who do not have anything obvious to give you in your career. Socrates said that a society is known by how it treats its weakest citizens. Nowhere else on Earth does that dictum guide a society more than in Japan, where the elderly are revered for their experience and wisdom.

In Japan it is said that you are still a junior citizen and still wet behind the ears until you are 50 years old. Only when you reach 50 can you claim to be a *sensei,* or teacher, and only then if you have lived your life well to that point. This attitude, of course, has both its positive side and its negative. On the positive side, Japanese society has long been built on tradition, which is the basis for its stability, low crime rate, and work ethic. It also treats all elderly people with great dignity and respect, a sign of a truly advanced society in my view. On the negative side, however, the Japanese do not encourage their youth to expand and develop new ideas. On the contrary, they want their youth to follow in the traditions of their seniors. Hence, the business world can be very slow to develop innovation and new ventures. For example, there is no word in Japanese for *entrepreneur.* We in the West, especially in the U.S., are exactly the opposite: We encourage innovation and the development of new enterprises, most of which are done by people under the age of 50. In fact, in this country, most new businesses—and therefore most of the new jobs being created today—are coming from ventures begun by young entrepreneurs. These customs are changing in Japan, however. In fact, I have been asked to start teaching entrepreneurship at the country's largest college, Nihon University, along with my colleagues Dr. Yuichi Iwaki and Dr. Takashi Kiyoizumi in part to help encourage Japan's young businesspeople.

In any case, Japanese business leaders often gauge the measure of a person by how he treats the elderly and those of lower rank than himself. Even before I realized how important this rule was among the Japanese, I managed to benefit by following it.

Several years ago, I tried to assist in the financing of an American company by several Asian investors. I arranged a meeting between the company executives and a group of Japanese bankers. When the two parties met, the meeting could not have gone worse. Naturally, I felt responsible to both sides for what appeared to be a horrible mismatch between the potential investors and the company's CEO. By the end of the day I was devastated. The meeting had taken place in Philadelphia and on the train ride home, I sat alone. The silence between me and my guests was so heavy that it felt as if I were carrying the train to New York on my back. When we arrived at Penn Station, I found myself walking just a few steps ahead of my party. Suddenly, I saw a middle-aged blind woman who was trying to find her way through the crowded terminal. Forgetting myself momentarily, I approached the woman, introduced myself, and asked where she wanted to go. She gave me a Park Avenue address, which I told her was just a couple of blocks from my office.

I feel a certain connection with people who suffer with blindness because a niece of mine was born with advanced cataracts and glaucoma, which greatly impaired her sight. My wife and I have been active ever since in trying to help scientists and doctors find a cure for blindness. We also sit on the board of a charity for blind children. Hence, my natural sense of solidarity with people who suffer with this affliction.

"Could we walk?" the woman asked me.

"It's a beautiful spring day," I said. "Why not. Please wait here for a moment while I say good-bye to my business associates." Much to my amazement, my clients insisted on walking with me. Apparently, they wanted to escort me back to my office. The next thing I knew, I had this blind woman on my arm as four very serious Japanese businessmen walked solemnly behind us. By now, I had let go of the fact that the day had been such a disaster. In fact, I felt buoyant as we all strolled along Park Avenue under the bright spring sun.

About a month later, I was informed that the Japanese investors had wired the funds to the American company. They had decided to invest after all. I was utterly baffled, but could not politely ask why they had decided to invest until a few years later, when I was in Japan and able to talk privately with a junior member of the Japanese investment group. Still, even this approach required some tact, so I took my associate to a restaurant where the two of us proceeded to get a little drunk on numerous sakes and beers. Once the atmosphere was sufficiently convivial, I asked, "Why did Mr. Takagi [the company's executive vice president] go ahead with that investment?"

"My boss said he never expected to see a young American leave us to assist a stranger who needed help," he said. "That impressed him. He said he expected you to give our company the same respect and courtesy that you gave that stranger."

It wasn't my business skills that solidified the deal, but certain human values that these investors and I shared: A desire to be treated in a certain way, especially when the chips were down, and a respect for people who seemingly are in a weaker position than ourselves. Such respect made them believe they could trust me, which was the basis for their risk.

* * *

Even though we in America do not have the same regard for the weak or the elderly—clearly a defect in our education—we nonetheless share the ideal that those lower on the company totem pole should be treated with respect and dignity. Not all of us follow that ideal, of course, but the vast majority of us know we should. I learned the importance of this value early in my career, when I was on the wrong end of the totem pole and working under someone who hadn't learned it as yet.

When I first came to Wall Street, I worked as a liaison between brokers and traders at E. F. Hutton. There I worked with many wonderful people, and one trader who was an abusive tyrant. He treated all liaisons in the office with arrogance and disdain. Rather than build up subordinates, he tore them down for his own egotistical gratification.

It wasn't long before I moved on, worked my way up "the Street," and eventually co-founded Paramount Capital, the venture capital corporation where I am the senior managing director. One day, my chairman, Lindsay Rosenwald, M.D., called me on the phone and said that he was considering hiring a new executive and wanted me to sit in on the interview. The interview had been underway some time when I entered Lindsay's office. Lindsay's desk faced me as I entered the room, and as Lindsay got up from his desk to introduce me, the man he was interviewing got up and turned around to greet me. In the instant we faced each other, a jolt of recognition ran between us like an electric current: It was none other than the tyrant from E. F. Hutton. The color drained from his face. I smiled, turned around, and walked out. The interview was over.

The moral of the story is this: Never abuse those below you, no matter what their position may be. They may not be your juniors for very long, and the web of life can be a minefield of irony. Or, as Bill Gates, chairman of Microsoft, once put it, "Be nice to the nerds. Chances are you'll end up working for one."

BE GRATEFUL: IT CHANGES EVERYTHING

In this country, we are very future-oriented, which is good in many respects. It is one of the reasons we are so inventive and creative. It is also partly why we have accomplished so much in virtually every field of endeavor. We push ourselves and in the process we create the future. But being focused on the future also has its dark side. It causes us to focus on what we don't have, but want, rather than appreciate what we have and all that we have been given.

When you think about what you want, you can't help but feel the emptiness caused by the lack of the thing you desire. That emptiness can change your feeling about what you have and all that you have accomplished. That can be a very big problem. It can make you critical of yourself and others. It can change the way you deal with time, especially how much time you give your loved ones and friends. You can devote less time to activities that have nothing to do with your job or income. In short, it can prevent you from giving your love and enjoying your life.

The one thing that changes all of this is gratitude. Sometimes, you've got to relax and think about all you have been given and all that you have accomplished, especially against tremendous odds. Sometimes, we all have to stop and give thanks.

Gratitude Is the Basis for Satisfaction in Business and in Life.

My parents did not have much money when my two brothers and I were growing up. Even after we were grown, my father averaged about $40,000 a year and my parents never went on vacation while we were kids. It wasn't until I attended college and saw them paying for my education that I realized how much they had sacrificed for my brothers and me. Yet, my parents always seemed financially satisfied with what they had. In fact, my father stressed how grateful they were to have a backyard. They never compared themselves to others (at least I didn't see it) and we always seemed to have enough. On one occasion, I even remember my father giving a neighbor who had gone bankrupt an interest-free loan.

One of the things my father used to say to me was that he knew the difference between "needs" and "wants." "The big difference between people today and those of us who grew up during the Depression," my father once told me, "is that, today, your wants have become your needs." A great many people today confuse the two, he said, believing that they "need" every new product that's advertised, as if it were important to their survival. As my father pointed out, that makes for a lot of frustration, dissatisfaction, and unhappiness. And all of it flows from a basic lack of gratitude for what we have.

Sometimes it's a worthwhile endeavor to think about how many of our actual needs, as well as wants, have been met and exceeded. Every so often, sit down on your sofa or in a private room and write down all the things you are grateful for in your life. Also, realize that most—if not all—of what you have achieved and acquired did not have to flow to you. Things could just as easily have gone the other way.

I often think that nothing I have accomplished actually had to happen. There were no guarantees. More important, every single project that I have undertaken has been incredibly delicate. Each endeavor contained that critical moment when everything could have fallen apart and collapsed in failure. Somehow, things came together, but in each case it required a certain magic. It's important to acknowledge that magic, as well as its source, whatever you think that may be. When we think about all that could have gone wrong, and when we write about our gratitude for all that went right, we are one step closer to answering Einstein's question in the affirmative.

HELP THOSE IN NEED

Beginning when I was very young, I had a speech impediment that caused me to stutter. As you no doubt understand, stuttering caused me a world of pain and embarrassment growing up. I never wanted to be called on in class, or to speak in a group, or to speak to an authority figure. Even communicating with my friends could be very difficult and humiliating. Interestingly, when I was in the third grade at Martin Avenue School in Bellmore, Long Island, New York, there was a girl in my class who stuttered even worse than I did. I was Shakespeare compared to her. And I cannot tell you the compassion I felt for that little girl. She taught me that no matter how bad things are, there is always someone worse off than you.

That same year, I had a teacher named Barbara Johnson. Ms. Johnson, as I called her, was a beautiful woman, tall and slender, with short brown hair and big, understanding eyes.

Ms. Johnson was getting a master's degree in education from Hofstra University and was specializing in speech. She took a special interest in me. She wanted to train me to stop stuttering. Every Saturday, Ms. Johnson took me to Hofstra University in Long Island where she was getting her graduate degree, and where she would help me learn to communicate better. Then she took me out to lunch where the lessons would continue. For every step of progress I made, she would reward me with a little piece of candy, an ice cream, a soda, or some other treat. For all I knew, Ms. Johnson was working with a half dozen other children, including the girl in my class who was also stuttering. But for me, Ms. Johnson was special. She had the warmest smile I had ever encountered. Naturally, I was completely taken with her. Under her guidance, I made tremendous progress with my speech and a few years later I was finally free of the problem. I vowed that if I ever became a teacher, I would have at least one-tenth of her integrity. She never charged my family one dollar for her time or expertise. Today, I regularly give presentations before large audiences, and I continue to think about that beautiful woman who helped to give me back my confidence.

Ms. Johnson gave me something else. She trained me to recognize something good and generous in people that would turn up again and again in my career.

When I first started out with an investment firm, I had a boss by the name of Charlie Murphy who ran the office at E. F. Hutton in Binghamton, New York, and became one of my most important mentors. Every week, an elderly woman used to come into our office off the street, read the newspaper, drink coffee, use the copying machine and the telephone, and then leave whenever the spirit moved her. She was always dressed poorly and, frankly, she didn't seem entirely competent. I thought for a long time that she was homeless. I never said anything about her sudden appearances. All I did was observe her presence, the various activities she engaged in, and her slightly oddball behavior. Charlie Murphy was well aware of her presence. Sometimes he would even greet her pleasantly by name. This went on for months. One day, curiosity got the best of me. I had to know why Charlie was letting this homeless person use the office as if it were her own.

"She isn't homeless, Peter," Charlie said with a smile. "Her name is Doris. She lives in the neighborhood. She has nowhere else to go."

As it turned out, Doris had had a small investment with Charlie many years before, which is how they met. In the process, she became friendly with Charlie, but as she aged she had become forgetful and slightly senile. Apparently, she had come to think of the investment office as her own business and Charlie as the manager who was running things for her. Charlie played along. It didn't hurt anyone, he said, and it did a lot for Doris. "As you know, Doris keeps to herself and we can afford the copying paper and the telephone costs. Sometimes you've got to do things for people just because it's good for them and the neighborhood in which you work," Charlie said. We never spoke about Doris again, but every time I saw her—or thought about her in the years since I left Hutton—I marveled at Charlie's generosity and his sage-like attitude toward others.

Like several people I have worked with over the years, Charlie understood that when you achieve success, you've got to find ways of giving back to others. With success comes a greater responsibility for caring for others. I am reminded of

President John F. Kennedy's famous quote from the Bible in which he said, "To whom much has been given, much is expected." He said this to remind Americans of their responsibility to the world and to each other.

In the East, it is said that when a stalk of wheat is young and arrogant, it stands up straight and holds its head up high. But when it is fully mature, it turns its head downward and becomes humble. At that point, the wheat is ready to be harvested so that it can nourish us all.

Charlie Murphy was one of the first people in business who taught me that success brings with it a responsibility to help others. Another man who knows this well is Aaron Feuerstein, the owner of Malden Mills, a textile manufacturer in Lawrence, Massachusetts.

On December 11, 1995, Malden Mills burned to the ground. In a single night, most of the company's 3,100 employees were out of work. Come morning, everyone in Lawrence knew that it wasn't just 3,000 people and their families who were about to face financial hardships. Without the mill and the money its employees spent in Lawrence, most of the town's other businesses—its grocery and clothing stores, gasoline stations, and the shops at the local mall—all would be in trouble. Many would be forced to close. The local officials of Lawrence, a city in the eastern part of Massachusetts not far from Boston, knew that the city was on the brink of ruin—and it was happening just two weeks before Christmas!

As every businessperson knows, a fire, especially a devastating one, can cause owners to rethink their entire operation. Do they rebuild in the same town, where labor is expensive, or do they relocate their factory overseas, where cheap labor can help create higher profits? Aaron Feuerstein, the owner of Malden Mills, faced those same questions. He knew how much economically strapped Lawrence depended on him and his employees; he also knew how much the 3,000 needed their jobs.

Feuerstein, whose grandfather started Malden Mills in 1907, didn't take long to announce his decision. That morning, as he walked through the rubble that was once his thriving factory and contemplated the many lives that hung in the balance, he announced that he would rebuild Malden Mills right where he was standing. Meanwhile, he wasn't going to let his employees starve while he rebuilt the factory. He decided to pay every employee his or her regular salary for months after the fire destroyed his business. He even issued Christmas bonuses!

"There was no question about the decision that I had to make," Feuerstein said later. "There was no way that I was going to take 3,000 people and throw them into the street and there was no way that I was going to condemn Lawrence to economic oblivion."

Feuerstein did this even before he knew if his insurance would support the rebuilding of his business. In fact, it would take another 18 months before the insurance company did in fact agree to cover Malden Mills' losses. Even before the insurance company's decision, however, Feuerstein had already started rebuilding. But by then, news of his decision and his magnanimity had gained a lot of admiring and powerful friends—not the least of which was President Clinton, who invited Feuerstein to sit next to him at his 1996 Inauguration; secretary of Labor Robert Reich, who helped shepherd the Labor Department's $1 million grant to help get the rebuilding off the ground; Massachusetts Senator Edward Kennedy; and much of the religious community of Boston, including Cardinal Bernard Law, who compared Feuerstein's commitment to "fundamental social justice" to the work of Mother Teresa.

When Malden Mills opened the doors to its $130-million state-of-the-art textile mill in September 1997, there was jubilation throughout Lawrence. Feuerstein, who was 71 at the time, thanked God and quoted the Bible in his speech to 30,000 people who attended the festivities. "All I can say is that each person must do his part, and hope they influence others," he said.

Feuerstein went on to become an example of what a man or woman should be when he or she achieves success and position in life. He has given talks before the student bodies of dozens of colleges and universities. He's been the keynote speaker at large conventions and gatherings of business leaders from all over the country. And he's addressed many grammar school classes to talk about ethics and values for living. After one such talk, a young student told a *Boston Globe* reporter that if he were in Aaron Feuerstein's position, he would have known the right thing to do, too, but he doubts he would have had the courage to do what Feuerstein did.

Aaron Feuerstein has emerged as a leader of conscience and vision, and he has done it by plucking the strings on the inherent values all of us have written in our hearts.

In the end, values define who we are as people and whose company we keep. I am reminded of what Mahatma Gandhi once said to a reporter. Gandhi was getting on a train as a reporter ran up and begged him for a quote. "Do you havse a message for my readers?" the reporter called out to Gandhi as he got on the train. Gandhi took out a pencil and scribbled something onto a small slip of paper. He handed it to the reporter and then disappeared onto the train. The paper read: "My life is my message."

The same is true of all of us.

CHAPTER

There Is
No Success
Without Failure

Many men go fishing all of their lives without knowing
that it is not fish they are after.
—Henry David Thoreau

I started working on Wall Street when I was 21 and by the time I was 30 I had made what most people would agree was a small but significant fortune. It was short-lived, however. In no time, I lost virtually all of it. What made the loss especially difficult was that my setback was due entirely to my own poor judgment. No one had squandered my success but me.

This was the first really big failure I had encountered in business. Still, I was young, confident, and eager. I would make it all back, I told myself. Three years later, I had made five times the money that I had lost as a 30-year-old. I was rich—at least on paper. Within a matter of several months, I lost all of that, too. Not only was I returned to my former humble means, but I realized that I was stupid. I had failed utterly and completely, I told myself. In truth, I hadn't just failed myself, but I had failed my family, the people I cared about outside of my family, and the many other people—including those who worked with me—who also might have benefited from my success. I felt as if I had let the whole world down, especially my wife, Donna. Fortunately for me, my wife was never much attached to the kind of success I dreamed about. Thank God, she never stopped believing in me. I could not say the same for myself. For a while, I doubted my judgment and my skills as a businessman.

Failure made me examine my character and my soul like nothing else had ever done in my life. Who am I? I wondered. What are my strengths and, more important, what are my weaknesses? Where did I go wrong—not once, but twice? What deep-seated arrogance and immaturity propelled me to be so cavalier at precisely the moment when I had reached the pinnacle of my career? What should I have done differently? If I get another chance at success, how should I behave to ensure that my success will endure? What are my real goals in life? Finally, I wondered: What is the purpose and meaning of failure, and how should I react to it?

As it turned out, this period was one of the richest and most educational times of my life. Yes, I have had many successes since then. But I would never have had them, I believe, if I had not failed so spectacularly early on. Looking back over my life, I realize that failure is an essential ingredient of success. In fact, I no longer believe in failure—at least not the way most people define it. In our culture, people think of failure as a static condition, a terminal point, in which one's inability to achieve one's aims, desires, or goals becomes apparent. It is seen as a more or less permanent condition. That is a completely erroneous understanding of failure.

During the past decade, I have carefully examined the lives of highly successful people and found that all people who succeed go through periods of their lives when all their efforts seem to fail. The difference between a successful person and someone who is unsuccessful is not failure—they both have plenty of that—but how they respond to difficult times. Today

I realize that life is a wave pattern—there are ups and downs, good times and bad. Life doesn't stop at any one point on the wave. Success and failure are just words that we use to describe different points on the wave. Wherever you may find yourself on the wave, know that it is temporary. There will be plenty of ups and downs to come. People maintain their general life circumstances—either as failures or successes—by what they fundamentally believe about themselves. From our beliefs about ourselves flow our judgment and actions.

Consider the life of Abraham Lincoln, who is widely regarded by historians as the greatest American President. Few nations ever produce a leader of Lincoln's character, understanding, and vision. Yet, prior to becoming president in 1860 at the age of 51, Lincoln's résumé read like one long list of failures. In 1831, his business failed. The following year, he ran for the Illinois State Legislature and lost. He decided to go into business again and watched his new enterprise flop. In 1835, his fiancé died and a year after that he suffered a nervous breakdown. In 1843, he ran for Congress and lost. Five years later, he ran again and lost again. In 1855, he ran for the U.S. Senate and was defeated; a year later he ran for Vice President and lost again. In 1859, he ran for the Senate again and lost again. In 1860, he became the 16th American president.

People don't remember Lincoln for his failures, of course, but for his greatest successes: holding together a nation that was being pulled apart by competing belief systems and economies, and for giving freedom back to African-Americans. As Lincoln's life demonstrates, failure doesn't define a man or woman so much as what he or she does after he or she experiences it.

There is a kind of formula for success, however. Or to put it more accurately, there is an approach to life that raises the likelihood of success. An essential part of that secret to success is how we behave when the events seem darkest and most despairing, when our lives seem out of control. That is the moment when success and failure are really determined. That is the moment when mysterious things begin to happen, when the web of life starts to weave its magic.

We start to understand the web of life by examining our own failures and successes, as well as those of others. Let me begin by telling you the details of some of my own failures, including my two biggest business failures. I'll also share some of the failures of other highly successful people, and show how they turned those apparent failures into great success.

THE LONG HAUL TO THE TOP OF THE MOUNTAIN, AND THE FAST RIDE DOWN

In the summer of 1989, the whole world seemed well within my reach. I had helped to finance a biotech company that was developing several new compounds that analysts believed had the potential to have significant sales. I agreed to help raise capital for the company based on its lead drug, which it was about to market. I received shares of stock in the company.

There was a lot of discussion about my raising the money, because I was young and inexperienced. What could I possibly know about picking a winner, many argued.

Two of those people were my own parents. Under SEC regulations, it's not permitted for immediate relatives of a Wall

Street broker or venture capitalist to invest at an IPO, or initial public offering. However, it's perfectly sound for a broker or banker to encourage those closest to him or her to buy stock after the company's shares are being publicly traded, or what is called the "after market." Once I raised the money and the company went public, I told my parents about the deal and how good this might get. "Buy some of this stock," I told them. "I think it's going to do very well."

"Yeah, yeah," they told me. But they never did it. I interpreted their reluctance as a lack of confidence in me. I was their son, after all. I was only 28. What could I possibly know?

Of course, my parents weren't alone. I was turned down by 100 investors before I managed to get a single person to invest in this company. I persevered and eventually I managed to get two firms—one American and the other Japanese—to invest most of the money the company needed. To be sure, there were many other smaller but still significant investors in the company. Anyway, I put the deal together; we created a new company around this new drug; we did the IPO, and we were launched.

The stock opened at about $1 a share and within 18 months had gone all the way to $15 a share. At that point, my investors and I had made a significant ROI, or return on investment. I was euphoric, to say the least. Not only had I successfully put my first big deal together, but that deal had succeeded beyond anyone's wildest dreams. I was also vindicated. All those potential investors who had turned me down because I was young and green could now see in *The Wall Street Journal* every day what they had missed. I had also proven myself to my parents, which was no small event in my life, either. They finally saw me as a skilled businessman and venture capitalist. But more important than anything else, I saw myself as a talented person who was capable of making things happen. I held myself in an entirely new light. It wasn't just because I had money suddenly, because in fact I was not doing all that badly before the deal struck gold. What mattered more to me was that I realized that I could do this work, that I could recognize opportunity—which is no small talent in itself—and convince people to invest very large sums of money in a very speculative venture. And then, as if all of that weren't enough, I saw that I could fulfill my promise to investors.

Now the truth is, you never promise success to any of your investors at the outset of a deal, even if they are large investors, or what are called accredited investors, which means someone who has had a salary of at least $200,000 for two years and/or $1 million in liquid net worth. It's illegal and immoral to make any promise of success. No one knows what will happen with any company or stock. Highly trained and educated people take their best guess. That's all they can do. What you do promise, however, is that your investors' money will go to exactly what they had invested in; that you will keep them fully informed at every step in the development of the deal; and that you will do all you can to create the success you had all hoped for. That's it. You can't do anything more than that. But after we had succeeded, I felt that I had taken people's money and made them even more money. That's a magical feeling. In some way, I had been part of a process in which people had placed enormous resources at risk and then succeeded beyond their hopes. And I had helped to make that happen.

I didn't have a chance to tug pridefully on my suspenders for too long before the stock started to plunge. "Oh my God," I said to myself one day, as I watched the stock start to sink. In fact, I knew in advance that the water was about to get rough because there had been some bad publicity surrounding the company and its new drug. I just didn't think it would fall that fast. I told my investors that if they wanted to sell, they should do it. At that point, I said, all they would lose was some of what they had gained on the stock. They would not have lost their original investment. There were a number of significant investors who wanted to stay with the stock, however. I was one of them, of course. As it turned out, that was a mistake.

When the wind finally stopped blowing, the stock had fallen from $15 a share to $2. Some people had lost a lot of money, which I felt terrible about. I also felt absolutely horrible about my own losses, but not for the reasons you might think. Yes, I suffered the fact that I was now a regular guy again with a less-than-impressive salary. I wasn't rich anymore. All of that deflated me like a screw in a bad tire. But more than that, I realized that it wasn't just *my* money. It was my wife's money. It was the money for my children's education. It was also the money that would have supported those who worked with me and whose lives would have been changed for the better by it. Before things went badly, it had appeared that we had all succeeded together. Now we were all sinking together. I had let people down. I should have sold when the stock was still high but the trend was clear. Instead, I had held on, even when the signs were obvious. I was arrogant and foolish, I told myself. For a while, I was glum.

But I'm not the type who stays down for long. It's not my personality. I started all over the following Monday morning and did the same things I had been doing: putting together new deals and working hard for success. In the meantime, I never sold the stock. There was no point to selling it, I decided. It had hit rock bottom. I might as well hold on to it and sell when it climbs a little bit. For a long time, the stock just sat there and did little or nothing—small increases followed by small declines. But in 1992, it gradually started to climb again until, in the summer of '94, the stock hit $40 a share. Wow! Who would have ever guessed that this stock, which had been dead in the water, would rebound beyond anyone's wildest expectations.

Needless to say, I was now a relatively wealthy young man. Not only was I rich, but I was vindicated. All the same feelings that I had had three years before were back and then some. When everyone had lost their heads and jumped off the horse, I had stayed in the saddle. I was a visionary, a sage. And now I was being rewarded for my good judgment. All those little doubts that still lurked inside me like small but still-painful wounds were now bathed in healing waters of my success. People at my firm complimented me on how smart I was for sticking with a stock that most believed had been nearly worthless. One of my friends at Paramount Capital offered me some different advice, however.

"Sell now, Peter," he said. "You'll never get a chance like this again."

I decided not to listen to his wise counsel. I thought the stock would go to a hundred. Little did I know that things were about to change.

News reports about health problems associated with the company's drug suddenly surfaced. The stock plunged—fast. You know, it takes a long time to walk from the second floor to the 40th, but it only takes a few seconds to get back down if you jump out the window. That's essentially what this stock did. It fell like a body from a great height.

Three months later, I lost 90 percent of what I had gained. I was humbled again. How was it possible to be so stupid? I wondered. Didn't you learn anything from your last failure? Weren't you the one who said that you would sell to preserve your success—and the success of those around you? Yes, but I wasn't really listening then, was I? When the stock started climbing again, I thought it foolish to sell before it peaked at 100 or better.

As I contemplated my folly, I remembered a quote from Baron Rothchild, who gave this reply when he was asked how he made his fortune. Said the banker: "I always sold too early."

LIFE LESSONS THAT LEAD TO SUCCESS

My failure precipitated another long bout of self-reflection. Only this time, it was much deeper and more serious. I didn't engage in a lot of self-pity. Instead, I took responsibility for my actions. What am I good at in this business? Where are my strengths? Perhaps more important, where are my weaknesses and blind spots? I wondered. How can I structure my professional life in order to maximize my talents and skills and get the support I need in the areas where I am weakest?

When I started to ask myself these and other related questions, I started to grow from my experience. That's when I started to become successful. I realized that my strength is seeing opportunities in business, raising money, and structuring deals. I can inspire investors, gain capital, put companies together, and take them all the way to success. But I'm not a good trader. I don't know when to sell. Once a company achieves success, I have to step aside and let a skilled trader take over the maintenance of that stock—even for my own portfolio.

In today's market, in which you can buy stocks on the Internet and essentially be your own broker, everyone thinks he or she is a genius with stocks. But one of the things that separates the average Jane or Joe from a professional trader is knowing when to hold on and when to get out. Great traders know when to sell. There's a science and an art to that part of the market. And the truth is, I don't have a talent for it. As a venture capitalist, I have always maintained the ethic that mine should be the first money in and the last money out of a deal. I have always believed that I have to be in the same boat as my investors. I feel that I must demonstrate to people that I so thoroughly believe in what I am doing that I will not bail out on them, or the company I have helped support or create, especially when the going gets a little rough. In fact, that's how I really feel. I believe in what I am doing.

But that's not the ethic of a good trader. One stock is as good as another to a talented trader. All he or she is interested in is performance and in preserving a person's assets. That is exactly the approach people need when it comes to success on Wall Street.

I remember meeting one of the greatest traders ever, the legendary Ace Greenberg, who once told me a little story about succeeding on Wall Street. Twenty years ago, Ace was playing bridge at the same table with Milton Petrie, one of the great retailers and philanthropists of the 20th Century. Milton asked Ace if he knew anything about Dome Petroleum, a Canadian oil company whose shares were publicly traded.

Ace replied, "I know a lot about it."

Milton said, "Oh, tell me what you know."

Ace said, "I know how to buy it and I know how to sell it. Which do you want me to do?"

Milton said, "Buy me $25,000 worth of shares."

Now, to the average Joe or Jane, that story is cute but pretty much meaningless. But to a person who understands Wall Street, that story tells it all. Ace Greenberg was saying that he had absolutely no attachments to any company beyond its performance on the stock market. Moreover, he knew exactly when to buy a stock and when to sell it so that his client made money. That is a great talent. Those who know when to buy and when to sell are going to make money, no matter whether the market is bullish or bearish. Milton Petrie was a sophisticated man who understood what Ace was saying. Which is why he immediately told him to buy $25,000 worth of stock.

One of the things I urge people to do today is this: When a stock succeeds, take the original investment off the table, by which I mean, get your money out of the deal and let your profits stay in the market. That way you're protected from any great losses. If the stock goes above two times your original investment, take out the amount equal to your original investment, so that you've essentially doubled your money, and let the rest of your profits above that stay in the market. In this way, you're always getting something back and you're protected against losses.

Today, I concentrate on what I do best and let my trader do what he does best. I have been very happy with the results. No matter what your business is, it's essential to know your strengths and weaknesses. You know, it's legally permissible for a medical doctor to practice any medical specialty, which means that a cardiovascular surgeon can practice neurology, or a general practitioner can be a urologist. They don't do it, though. Why? Because no one can be good at every aspect of their profession and being a doctor carries with it so much responsibility and requires so much knowledge that it would be impossible to practice all forms of medicine. If a doctor is going to be good at his profession, he must specialize in order to know all that he must know within the area of his expertise. (More about all of that in Chapter 7.)

The same is true of business. No one is good at every aspect of his or her business. Real power and success come from knowing your strengths and weaknesses and creating a circle of support around you that maximizes one and compensates for the other.

One of the things I learned from my own failures is to hire people whom I perceive are smarter than I am—especially in the areas where I am weak. Once I have done that, I pay them well and let them do what they do best. You have to give people the chance to succeed by letting them do what they are good at. Like most professions, business is teamwork. It is collaborative. If it's a one-man show, you can almost guarantee failure.

FAILING ALL THE WAY TO SUCCESS

There's an old saying that, if you always do what you always did, you will always get what you always got.

I believe that most of us will go right on doing what we have always done, unless we fail in some obvious way. If we have a modest success, we tend to enjoy it and come to believe that bigger things are beyond us. In such circumstances, we never come to understand what is keeping us back, or keeping us from realizing more of our potential. But when we fail, we are forced to change and grow, which makes us wiser, stronger, and better able to succeed.

There's no better illustration of this than Pete Sampras, who, next to Rod Laver, is without doubt the greatest tennis player of all time. No one who has ever picked up a tennis racquet was more blessed with talent and potential than Pete Sampras. At the time of this writing, he has won 63 tennis titles and 13 Grand Slam events, the most grand slams of any other tennis player in the history of the game. Pete won his first grand slam title at the U.S. Open in 1990 at the age of 19. By his own admission, he wasn't ready for that kind of success. Nor was he prepared to sustain it. As he would later explain, Pete was prepared for a much more modest career, and much smaller achievements, at least until he experienced a crushing defeat in the finals of the 1992 U.S. Open against Stefan Edberg, the great Swedish player.

". . . Up until that point, I was happy being in the finals, quarters and semis at the slams," Sampras told *The New York Times* (July 11, 2000). "I was content just being top 10 in the world. But that match changed my career. It just finally showed me that I do hate to lose. Because I remember that match with Stefan Edberg, I gave in a little bit at the end and got a little soft. And months after that loss, it would just really [eat] away at me. I felt that I kind of gave it away." Pete later told CBS sports that he would never have won 13 grand slams if he hadn't lost that match against Edberg.

Failure made Sampras the champion he became. Defeat taught him the value of victory. It also taught him what it took to win. He realized that on some level he had allowed the failure to occur, or as he said, "I gave in a little bit at the end and got a little soft." He wasn't just the victim of another opponent; he was the victim of his own weakness. Because he was honest with himself, he saw himself in a new light and realized how he had to change in order to fulfill his potential.

The web of life, like a great gardener, uses failure to prune us and, in the process, to show us who we are, what we are doing, and how we have to change in order to succeed. In the end, failure can help us become the unique individuals we truly are. If you're unique, you cannot help but succeed.

Virtually everyone who succeeds in life has done so after experiencing some form of failure. As B.C. Forbes once said, "History has demonstrated that the most notable winners usually encountered heartbreaking obstacles before they triumphed. They won because they refused to become discouraged by their defeats." The question is, how should you respond to defeat in order to turn failure into success? After studying the lives of successful people, and reflecting deeply on my own experiences with turning failure into success, I have come up with five rules for doing exactly that. They are as follows:

PETER'S RULES FOR TURNING FAILURE INTO SUCCESS

RULE 1: Listen to your heart.

Before you react to your failure or loss, before you change anything about yourself, reflect on what you truly want. Once you know your heart's desire, never give up.

Failure is the greatest teacher you will ever have. Its first and most important lesson is presented to us as a question, which is this: What do you want to do with your life? Do you want to stay in the field or line of endeavor in which you just experienced failure, or is there another line of work for you?

These questions are not so simple as they seem, in part because failure always makes us doubt ourselves and stop believing, if only for a short while, in our goals, ambitions, and abilities. In the immediate aftermath of your apparent failure, postpone dealing with your doubts about your abilities or talents. Rather, confine yourself to the question of whether or not you really want this kind of job, or business, or if you truly want to fulfill this ambition.

If the answer is yes, ask yourself why. Sometimes we want something for all the wrong reasons. Perhaps we want to experience success in this area because it will give us status, or because someone else wants us to make this our life's path. You will never fully succeed, nor be happy with your life, if you are doing a job or engaging in a relationship because someone else wanted you to do such a thing. It's the surest road to misery.

I have worked with a lot of doctors in my life and I can tell you that a substantial percentage of them became physicians not because they truly wanted that profession, but because one or both of their parents wanted them to be doctors. It's the same with engineers, stockbrokers, businesspeople, and venture capitalists. People find themselves in careers that give them no deep satisfaction or pleasure. A great many of these people experience some form of mid-life crisis—a divorce, financial loss, or an illness—that gets them to reflect on their choices and career paths. In the midst of such a crisis, they ask themselves how they managed to dedicate themselves to a profession that they never enjoyed, nor wanted to be a part of. Crisis, or failure, is often a form of medicine that forces you to ask important questions that only you can answer for yourself. Such a crisis puts you back in touch with who you really are and what you really want in life. Failure puts you back in touch with your heart and soul.

Interestingly, in Chinese, the character for crisis also means opportunity. As the Chinese have long understood, the moment of crisis can also be a moment of tremendous transformation and opportunity, if you take the right approach.

I'm reminded of the story of Bernie Marcus and Arthur Blank, who were the managers of Handy Dan, Inc., a hardware and do-it-yourself home repair center. In 1972, Handy Dan went public, but in 1977 a recession hit and Handy Dan filed for Chapter 11 to reorganize and survive. In the process, the Handy Dan chairman decided to fire both Marcus and Blank. Both men were now on the street and neither had any money. They had to ask themselves what they really wanted to do. As it turned out, they liked the hardware business and both believed they could succeed in it, despite their recent failures. Recommitted, the two managed to raise enough capital to open a little hardware store they called Home Depot. That business, of course, went on to become the largest chain of hardware stores in the world. Not only did it make Marcus and Blank billionaires, but because they offered stock options to their employees, it transformed truck drivers, dock workers, and secretaries into millionaires, as well. At one point, Bernie Marcus's secretary's stocks alone were worth $6 million.

When I lost the money I had made in the stock market, I had to ask myself if this was the profession I wanted to spend the rest of my life in. For me, the answer was yes. But it wasn't without important caveats. I could not go on doing business in the same way. I could no longer be both a deal maker and a broker. I had the skills and talents for only one of those professions. That meant that I had to give up the job for which I was unsuited. In fact, once I did that, I felt free to be who I truly am. That was one of the most liberating experiences I had ever had in business.

Failure forced me to face myself and assess who I am, what I am good at, and what my weaknesses are. It taught me where I belonged and where I didn't. In the process, it redoubled my commitment to doing better. And it gave me a kind of rebirth of my professional life.

RULE 2: Listen to your critics.

Never measure yourself by your detractors' assessments, but listen and learn from their criticism.

This is one of the hardest and most mature things any adult can do: Listen to and reflect on the criticisms from others after you have experienced failure. Many successful businesses have learned this lesson, however. Both 3M and Procter and Gamble Company have long offered customers 1-800 complaint numbers so that the companies could hear from their customers where they were failing. We must know our weaknesses if we are to succeed.

Still, listening to the criticism of others is extremely difficult. For one thing, anyone can criticize another human being. It takes nothing to criticize. Any fool can do it and the bigger the fool, the more likely he is to criticize others. You probably recall the Bible story of Job, a good man who was unjustly subjected to great losses and terrible physical torments. Two of Job's so-called friends were all too happy to tell him again and again that his problems were all his own fault. Job endured terrible pain and the claptrap of lesser men. All of us have this same experience at some point in our lives.

Every time we fail, part of us feels like Job, the victim of an unjust universe. Instead of wallowing in such feelings, we must rally ourselves and listen to our critics to see if there is anything in their words that's worth considering. Perhaps something that is being said as criticism can help get us closer to our goals and ambitions. This is difficult, obviously, because failure wounds our pride and causes us to wall off those who would try to make us feel even worse than we already do.

Try not to let the messenger get in the way of the message. If we allow ourselves time to reflect, we will see the truth in some of the criticisms leveled against us. It may be that the web of life is attempting to get us out of some area where we don't belong and, in fact, will make us unhappy in the long run. Search for the lesson in failure. In the end, it will make you stronger and better able to succeed.

Herman Meier, Austrian Gold medalist in the 1998 Olympic downhill skiing championships, was cut from his 1990 ski team when he was only 16 because he was "too small" and weak to perform. Instead of sulking and hating the coach, Meier acknowledged to himself that the coach was probably right and that he would have to get stronger in order to achieve his dream of being a downhill racer. What did he do? He became a brick layer. Anyone who has ever seen him ski knows that the man is a powerhouse. Tall and muscular, Meier looks like a comic book hero on skis. In the 1998 Olympics, he lost his balance while traveling at more than 40 miles an hour and then lifted off the ground and flew more than 100 feet before he crashed into a snow fence and embankment. People hurried to his side, terrified that he had broken every bone in his body. He was fine, it turned out, and went on to win two gold medals in the '98 Winter Games.

Learning from failure is in itself a step in the process of transforming failure into success. This is how we learn about ourselves, about life, and about our professions. The thing we call failure is seen by many successful people as merely a learning step toward success. It took Thomas Edison 2,000 experiments before he invented the lightbulb. A young reporter, still wet behind the ears, asked him how it felt to fail so many times. Edison told the brash young man, "I have never failed once. I invented the lightbulb. It was just a 2,000-step process."

RULE 3: "Yes, you can."

That's the answer to 99 percent of people who ask if they can ever achieve their goals and ambitions. It's your answer, too. However, it's up to you to find the path to the realization of your goal.

After my wife and I got married, we very much wanted children, but we soon discovered that I had a low sperm count, which was preventing us from conceiving. I had had the mumps when I was a child and doctors speculated that that disease probably left me with low fertility. I spent the next two years consulting the best physicians in New York, as well as throughout the world, and every one of them told me to forget about having children. It would be impossible for us to conceive naturally with my sperm count. One doctor went so far as to suggest that I mix some of my two brothers' sperm with my own and then artificially inseminate my wife. "Why not?" the doctor said. "It's almost exactly the same set of genes." Obviously my wife vetoed that.

I kept thinking, there's got to be a way that I can improve my sperm count. "No," the smartest doctors in the world were telling me. "You can't do that." I continued searching. Finally, I found two doctors who thought they could help me, one in Florida and the other in Israel. Remarkably, both gave me essentially the same advice, which was this: Each day I should take between 400 to 800 International units of Vitamin E, 1000 mg. of vitamin C, a daily dose of liquid zinc, which I had to take from an eye dropper, and one or two kyolic garlic tablets. (It was odorless garlic, which meant that I could kiss while I was trying to conceive.) In addition, I should avoid all hot baths and hot showers and wear boxer underwear, as opposed to briefs. In six months, my sperm count had risen tenfold and within a year my wife, Donna, was pregnant. Today we have three healthy and beautiful children.

When we were first told that I had a low sperm count, I felt terrible that my wife would be deprived of having her own children because of my biological problem. To be honest, I felt somewhat inadequate and very much the failure. It would have been easy for me to accept the pronouncements of my doctors—they were the experts, after all—and either start adoption procedures, or give up entirely on the idea of having a family. I refused to do either. I believed that I could heal whatever problem I had and restore my sperm count. All I needed was the right advice. I would do the rest.

Every day we hear about people who cure themselves of diseases that doctors called incurable. I remember the story of Nathan Pritikin, a man with only two years of college, who in 1958 was told by his doctors that he had incurable heart disease. Pritikin, a successful businessman and inventor, was advised by his physicians to retire from his business and spend the remainder of his life resting. He was only 43 years old. Was there any way to cure heart disease? he asked his doctors. "No," they told him. The illness was caused by aging and stress, both of which were unavoidable, especially for a man who ran a large manufacturing company, as Pritikin did. That was the state of knowledge of heart disease in 1958. His doctors were adamant: If he continued his active life, he would die young.

Pritikin had had a long interest in health and nutrition and knew that there was some scientific evidence that linked diet and exercise to heart disease. He investigated further, found more scientific support for his hypothesis, and decided to create his own program for diet and exercise to cure his disease.

In 1959, he went to nutrition experts at UCLA and told them that he wanted to lower the fat and cholesterol content of his blood. When the nutritionist asked him why, he said, "Because I believe that fat and cholesterol may be the causes of heart disease."

The nutritionist thought he was crazy. Lowering the fat and cholesterol levels of your blood is probably impossible, the UCLA nutritionist said. Besides, reducing foods that are high in fat and cholesterol is dangerous, he was told. They're the best foods you can eat. Faced with the fact that there was no diet for heart disease, he invented one himself.

In 1961, he started running to boost his fitness and strengthen his heart. This was long before there was any running craze or even running shoes. Pritikin ran in his street shoes, which was an odd sight along the winding streets in his hometown of Santa Barbara, California. "People used to stop their cars along the side of the road and ask me if everything was all right," he recalled many years later. "They thought that I was running from some kind of trouble."

Not only did he look odd, but his shoes provided him no support and caused his knees to hurt. When he went to his doctor and told him he was running, his doctor thought he was crazy. "People over 40 can't run," one physician told him. The medical reason: His knees would wear out. Faced with the fact that he wanted to run, and that there were no running shoes, he decided to invent such a shoe himself. Pritikin went to a sneaker manufacturer and had a special shoe made to support his legs and feet as he ran. After that, he had no more knee problems.

Time after time, Pritikin came up with ideas that were long before their time. Every time he had such an idea, leading experts of the time rejected his notions as foolish. Yet, he persevered and eventually created a diet and exercise program that cured him of his heart disease. Once he did that, he opened the Pritikin Longevity Center in Santa Monica, California, that helped to cure tens of thousands of people of heart disease, high blood pressure, adult-onset diabetes, and many other serious and even life-threatening diseases. He wrote several best-selling books as well, which reached millions. Nathan Pritikin changed the way heart disease was treated in the U.S. and around the world. He did it because he had a problem that he insisted had a solution.

* * *

It's in the nature of things that our dreams are confronted by obstacles. Don't ask me why. I don't know. All I know is that it's the way things are. Our job is to overcome the obstacles and the many failures we meet along the way.

Many people believe that the single greatest obstacle to their dreams is money. People tell me all the time that they have a great business idea, but lack the capital to create it. In nine cases out of ten—or perhaps 99 out of 100—that's not the real problem. If you have a dream you believe in, you can raise the money yourself, or start your enterprise on a shoestring. The "little" companies listed below were all started on less than $10,000.

Apple Computer

Mary Kay Cosmetics

Lillian Vernon

The Limited

Dell Computer

Gateway 2000

Papa John's Pizza

Nantucket Nectars

Ernest and Julio Gallo

Hard Candy

Microsoft

Needless to say, money was not the reason they got off the ground, nor was it the reason they became great success stories. A number of those enterprises, as you know, are *Fortune* 500 companies today, but even the smaller ones are impressive for their creativity and their success.

Our answers are out there. Solutions are waiting to be found. However, there is no substitute for searching earnestly, sincerely, with the clear intention of finding your answer.

RULE 4: Pay the price.

Here's a fundamental fact about life: Multiple failures are the price of success. Get used to it.

Once you've identified your goal, and you see the path to its attainment, you must be willing to dedicate yourself to the realization of your ambitions. That will mean that you will experience failure on your way to success. Don't stop. Keep going. When used properly, failure is an experience that trains and sharpens your skills; it tempers your soul, making you stronger and better able to do the job or reach the goal that you have set for yourself. Mark McGwire is a wonderful example of exactly this process.

Mark McGwire, the man who broke Roger Maris's record of 61 home runs in a single season, was nearly convinced that he was washed up as a baseball player in 1991. Near the end of the season, he went to his manager, Tony LaRusso, and asked him not to put him in the lineup, lest he continue making outs and have his batting average fall below .200. LaRusso agreed and McGwire finished the season with an average of .201— dismal by any professional baseball player's standards, but absolutely horrendous for a star like McGwire. What was nearly as bad for him was that he managed to hit only 22 home runs that year.

During the off-season, McGwire seriously considered retirement. Some part of him believed he was finished as a ball player. Instead of quitting, however, he worked hard on his swing and his concentration and returned the next year with a renewed commitment to excel. The following season, he hit .268, with 42 home runs.

McGwire was back, or so it seemed. Unfortunately, the tough times had just begun. The following year, he was hit by a series of injuries again. In the 1993 season, McGwire played only 74 games and remained on and off the injured reserve list for the next six years. McGwire spent more time in rehab than he did at the plate. As injury after injury sidelined him, as he re-entered rehab and got back in the game, McGwire became a study in perseverance and determination. Still, lots of people wondered why he bothered. Many advised him to quit the game. He was finished, they said, through. Give it up already, you're making a spectacle of yourself. (Like Job, McGwire was also followed by a chorus of fools.)

Still, even his detractors had to admit that his swing of the bat was poetry in motion and the power with which he hit the ball caused professional baseball players throughout the league to watch him in awe as he took batting practice before a game. No one since Ruth himself had a swing like that, many believed. McGwire could hit the ball so far out of the park that rival players often found themselves gawking in admiration. Many couldn't suppress a bout of the giggles when McGwire let one fly.

Of course, then came 1998 and that remarkable season when it all came together for this man. He hit 70 home runs and broke Maris's record. It wasn't just what he did, but how he did it. McGwire was a man of tremendous dignity and nobility, having transcended so much injury and frustration to become one of the greatest hitters baseball had ever seen.

"You're looking at a guy who turned his career around because I could have walked away from the game," he said later. "I could have stuck my head in a hole and never been heard from again. So, I'm a perfect example of a player who has dealt with so much adversity—injuries, playing terrible—but then working hard, climbing that mountain and reaching the peak."

His manager, Tony LaRusso, was amazed at all McGwire had accomplished. "Even if it was just the baseball side, it would be really significant and impressive," LaRusso said. "But you think about the injuries and the rehabilitations, that he overcame those things. I think it's even stranger than fiction what this man has done."

RULE 5: Have faith in yourself, in your efforts, and in the web of life.

Life is a wave pattern. There are ups and downs. What we call failure is merely a point on the wave. That point's location is the trough of the wave, the low point. The energy of that wave will send you upward, especially if you are doing all you can to succeed. As the wave rises, little things begin to happen that propel you forward. Very often, these opportunities are unexpected. I have found that if you give yourself totally to your cause, some unexpected magic arises to help you. What's really happening is that the wave is rising and you're riding it toward better things.

Therefore, whenever things go badly for you, give yourself some time; get away from the problem. After you have rested and feel able to devote yourself again to the adventure of your life, stay alert for the opportunities, the magic. The wave will rise and bring you with it.

A few years ago, I represented a company called Avigen that had developed gene therapy for an array of genetic disorders, including hemophilia and sickle cell anemia. Essentially, Avigen scientists had developed a way to safely carry medicines to genes by altering the genetic make-up of a virus that is already present in virtually everyone's bloodstream by the age of 5. This genetically altered virus, in effect, acts as a kind of limousine service for the medicine, which, once it's inside the cell, can repair the damaged genes that cause the illness. Studies had shown that related products created by this company could also be used in the treatment of prostate cancer. There was tremendous excitement among scientists over these new therapeutic tools. Unfortunately, the company was desperately in need of money and was on the brink of bankruptcy.

I believed that we could raise money in Japan and, along with the company CEO, John Monahan, Ph.D., I flew to Japan to talk to potential investors, some of whom I had done business with before. When we got there, I was informed that genetic research in Japan was against the law, which meant that Japanese businesspeople could not invest in companies that did such research.

Of course, Dr. Monahan and I were dejected, especially since it now appeared that his company would go out of business, despite the enormous potential benefits to millions of people that his company offered.

On the morning after we had been informed that genetic research was against the law in Japan, Dr. Monahan and I sat in a coffee shop, both of us dejected, and prepared to leave the country. I sat at the table, hunched over a Japanese newspaper that I was perusing for no other reason, it seemed to me, than to distract myself from my feelings of having made a terrible mistake. Little did I know that the web of life was at work right at that very moment.

Though I speak a little Japanese, I do not read a word of the language. As I turned the pages of the newspaper, I suddenly saw an illustration that grabbed my attention. It appeared to be a diagram of a virus that was carrying a molecule to a cell's genes. Below the illustration was a headline and below that a lengthy article. I jumped up from my seat and began asking people in the restaurant if they spoke any English. Eventually, I found a man who did and asked him what the headline and the article was about.

He took a minute to study the page. Then he said, "Oh, the Japanese Government approved genetic research yesterday. Before that, it was against the law. Now Japanese scientists can investigate these areas."

And Japanese businesspeople could invest in them!

Suddenly, Dr. Monahan and I were in business again. I made a series of telephone calls very quickly that morning and before long we had raised $10 million for Avigen. Within a year of raising that money, the company raised another $25 million. And Avigen stock went through the roof. When it first opened, Avigen was selling at $8 a share. Their various financial crises caused the stock to fall to $1 a share. But when we got the company on its feet and its scientists started to prove their approach even further in human trials, the stock went to $89 a share. Needless to say, there were a lot of happy people at Avigen. More important, we believe that within several years, Avigen may have a potential–long-term cure for hemophilia, sickle cell anemia, and other serious disorders.

The truth is that you can do all you can in a particular endeavor and still not have ultimate control over what happens in the end. That does not mean that we should do less than all we can. It just means that every deal, every endeavor, needs a little help from the web of life in order to succeed.

You're going to go through a lot in your life; you're going to be delivered from a lot of problems through no special effort of your own. When you are, think about those experiences long and hard. When you do, you'll realize that many times you thought that a particular day or week was going to be trouble-some, and yet when you got to that day, or you passed through that week, the events were not nearly so bad as you thought they were going to be. Somehow, the events came together to support you and to get you through the difficulty you thought might crush you. There was help. The web of life was support-ing you through a difficult time.

This is especially the case with failure. Virtually every fall is followed by a rise, every failure followed by success. Reflect on these experiences carefully. Discover the goodness and the love in life. Answer Einstein's question—Is the universe a friendly place?—with a resounding *yes*. Then failure is only a tempo-rary condition, an opportunity to learn. In fact, it is only a step on the path to success.

CHAPTER 4

The Anatomy of a Deal

*To win one hundred victories in one hundred battles
is not the acme of skill. To subdue the enemy
without fighting is the acme of skill.*

—Sun Tzu

*P*eople often imagine that business deals are struck between groups of people who are trying to put something over on each other. In fact, that is sometimes the case, especially when you have something that the other group wants so badly that they are willing to cheat you out of it. But in my experience, those kinds of deals never work out. Something causes them to fall apart, especially if you are willing to stick to your values. In the end, your dogged hold on your values and fundamental goals are what save you, but when things are going badly and all that you have worked for is threatened, the temptation to throw in with the wrong people can be overwhelming.

What follows is the anatomy of a deal, a very big and important deal involving the creation of a company that could provide the answers to diabetes and even cancer. The company's name is Keryx and on July 23, 2000, Keryx executives made their initial public offering (IPO) at $10 a share. The company was worth in excess of $200 million. Because the technology offered by Keryx has so much potential, and therefore is so valuable, we encountered a few sharks on our way across the water.

I was intimately involved in the creation of Keryx and helped raise much of the money to get it off the ground. Essentially, Keryx is a new drug company whose core technology is the capacity to influence how cells communicate with each other, a process called *signal transduction*. One of the pathways that facilitate communication between cells is a group of enzymes called *kinases*. Whole sequences of these enzymes, or kinases, serve as messengers between cells, and within cells, relaying information back and forth, much like a bucket-brigade does at a fire-fight.

Kinases are among the most important functions in the cell's efforts to maintain health. As long as they are functioning properly, a cell behaves normally, or as it should. Sometimes these enzymes become disrupted, however, causing cells to receive the wrong types of messages. When situations like that arise, cells behave inappropriately and oftentimes give rise to one or another illness, including diabetes and even cancer.

Scientists have been working for years on ways to influence these kinases. One of their goals, for example, is to stop the type of messages that stimulate cells to reproduce out of control, or become cancerous. By doing this, scientists hope to cure cancer and many other illnesses, including diabetes and heart disease. In the case of heart disease, scientists one day will be able to stimulate the creation of new tissue, including the growth of new blood vessels, and thus avoid the need for coronary bypass surgery. This process, called *angiogenesis,* can also be reversed, which will be important in the treatment of cancer. Scientists hope to block the formation of blood vessels to cancerous tumors; such a feat would starve tumors of blood and oxygen. Such a process, called *anti-angiogenesis,* is one of the most exciting new approaches to the cure for cancer.

Cancer, heart disease, and diabetes are not the only illnesses that can be effectively treated through the repair of
kinases. These enzymes can be manipulated to stimulate the
growth of stronger bones, more rapid healing, and even grow
hair on people who experience baldness as a consequence of
chemotherapy.

Dr. Morris Laster, a medical doctor on the staff of
Paramount Capital, teamed up with a group of scientists who
were in the late stages of developing a technology for both
inhibiting and stimulating kinases within cells. Their remarkable technology was being made possible, in part, by the discovery of the human genome, or the complete genetic map, which
allows scientists to know the correct kinase sequence, and thus
know the basis for healthy cellular communication. In addition
to knowing the correct kinase sequences, these scientists also
found ways to stop inappropriate commands, such as those
that produce cancer, and to repair broken sequences, such as
those that produce diabetes. Needless to say, this was among
the most exciting new discoveries to come out of biotechnology in a very long time and we, at Paramount Capital, were
right on the cutting edge of this new technology with our own
company, Keryx. As Paramount Chairman Dr. Lindsay
Rosenwald said, "It's not every day that you come across a technology that offers the real possibility of curing cancer."

But the path to the creation of Keryx was not an easy one.
In business, as in the rest of life, whenever you have something
good, there will be those who will try to take it from you. We
nearly lost Keryx twice.

Keryx came into being in October 1998, after many
months of hard work by Morris Laster, M.D., and Schmuel
Ben-Sasson, Ph.D., an Israeli scientist who was the inventor of

the technology that influences these kinase sequences. Dr. Ben-Sasson headed a team of scientists and physicians, all of whom were working on different aspects of the kinase puzzle.

Dr. Laster had happened upon Dr. Ben-Sasson and his work quite unexpectedly. Morris, who had worked in our offices for the previous two years, was employed at Paramount Capital to find new technologies that we might invest in and turn into successful companies. He moved to Israel where he opened his own company with the same purpose, never letting go of his affiliation with us, however. One of his employees happened upon Dr. Ben-Sasson's work, which was buried among an enormous stack of other seemingly worthwhile projects. Morris looked over the ideas presented by Dr. Ben-Sasson and immediately grasped the importance of his discovery. He telephoned Dr. Ben-Sasson and, after several meetings, the two decided to work together to create a new company that would fund the scientist's ground-breaking work.

In fact, Morris already had a history of recognizing important discoveries that others overlooked.

THE SERENDIPITOUS CREATION OF NEOSE

Morris Laster came to work with us in 1989 after reading an ad that we had placed for a medical doctor who could identify and evaluate new technologies that we might pursue as possible investment ventures. Morris was a fourth-year medical student who was taking some time off before going back to school to do his residency in surgery. He showed up for the interview with no business experience, nor any business background.

I'll never forget our interview with him, which was conducted by Lindsay Rosenwald and me. After talking extensively about Morris's experience at school and his plans for his future in medicine, Lindsay asked him, "Do you have any experience in business?"

"No," Morris said.

"Did you take any accounting courses in college?" Lindsay asked.

"No," Morris said.

"Any economics?"

"No," Morris said, shaking his head innocently.

"Any management courses?" Lindsay asked, as if searching desperately for some reason to support his intuitive fondness for Morris and his desire to hire him.

"No, no management either."

Lindsay was at a loss. I could tell he wanted to hire Morris badly, but could find no real basis for doing it.

Exasperated, he finally said, "Okay, listen. Something very big happened in the business world last week. Do you know what it was?" You could almost hear the hope in Lindsay's voice as he asked the question.

"Uh, let me see," Morris said, as he rubbed his chin. "Oh yeah, Drexel Burnham went out of business."

"That's right!" Lindsay said. "You're hired."

Morris was given an office, the necessary computer equipment, and turned loose on the world of biotechnology. He had one mandate: Find new technologies that might prove to be profitable business ventures for our firm.

By his own admission, Morris spent the next few months at Paramount Capital looking at the ceiling.

"I didn't know a thing about biotechnology or venture capitalism," Morris recalled years later. "I didn't even know where to start looking."

Meanwhile, there was a man in the adjoining office who was trying to do the same thing Morris was supposed to be doing, and enjoying about the same success. "He had a lot of projects going," Morris recalled. "But he was unable to close a single deal." Perhaps for this reason and his own fearful outlook on life, he was extremely distrustful of Morris. "He refused to talk to me. I'd say good morning or ask him a question and he refused to say anything to me," Morris recalled with a laugh. "He was absolutely paranoid of me. He didn't realize that I knew less than he did."

Occasionally, Lindsay would ask Morris to evaluate some new business plan or proposal that had recently fallen on his desk. Morris thought every one of them was a waste of time. "I may not have had any business experience," Morris said, "but I had common sense. I could see that these plans were not going to work."

Finally, after Morris had spent a couple of months treading water, his wife suggested that he start reading newspapers and business publications for possible leads on new technologies. Morris thought it was a good idea. Every day, he picked up *The Wall Street Journal* and *The New York Times* and read them assiduously. He also read all the business magazines and newspapers, such as *Forbes* and *Barons*.

In February 1990, Morris read a small but interesting article about a doctor at the University of Pennsylvania who had figured out how to synthesize sugars. Why was that important?

"No one had ever been able to do that before," Morris pointed out. Sugars, or *oligosaccharides* as they are often called, are involved in a wide array of cellular interactions and, in fact, influence how cells behave. They have unique roles in determining how and when cells divide, how the body responds to infection, how the body handles proteins, and other important functions. Sugars produced in breast milk play an essential role in infant development; they also help determine how strong the child's immune system becomes. "They are very complex chemistry," said Morris. "Because no one has ever been able to synthesize sugars, there's a lot about cellular function that we don't know. This new discovery could give us greater knowledge of the inner workings of cells. There are many possible products that might be developed as a result of this discovery."

Intrigued by the article, Morris decided to telephone the professor, whose name was Steve Roth, a 50-something scientist and chairman of the university's department of biology. Morris and Dr. Roth had an easy communication and after their initial talk the two decided to get together to talk about Roth's discovery over a few beers and several games of squash.

"I have found that business is based on human relationships," Morris said a decade later. "If you get together and you like each other, you can overcome a lot of hurdles." Morris and Roth hit it off immediately. They had a lot in common, most of which had nothing to do with business. "We're both very big sports fans," Morris said.

Not only did the two have a good rapport, but Morris could see the medicinal and financial value of Roth's discovery instantly. Roth's sugars could be used in a wide array of medicines and other commercial properties, including vaccines for melanoma and ovarian cancers.

As it turned out, Morris's ability to see the value in Roth's discovery was a rather remarkable insight. Many thousands of people had seen the same *Wall Street Journal* article that Morris had, but he was the only person who telephoned Roth to follow up on the professor's discovery.

There was no company when Dr. Roth and Morris Laster met. They were only two men with a mutual appreciation for what the other brought to the table. Roth had a unique scientific discovery. Laster had the ability to recognize the importance of that discovery; he also had the backing of our company, which was capable of raising the needed start-up funds. In April 1990, about two months after their initial meeting, Morris suggested to Roth that the two form a business to manufacture and market products based on Roth's discovery. Roth agreed.

At that point, the two entered into a delicate negotiation that actually involved three parties: Steve Roth, Morris Laster, who represented Paramount Capital, and the University of Pennsylvania, which had certain limited rights to Roth's discovery, as well. Based on coaching that Lindsay Rosenwald and I provided, Morris negotiated the deal.

With that, Morris, Roth, and the University of Pennsylvania started talking. The university had certain limited legal rights that gave it a minority ownership and a percentage of royalties on anything produced by their faculty members, including Dr. Roth. Since these rights were well-established, the real negotiation had to take place between Laster and Roth.

"This kind of negotiation depends, first, on knowing what everyone wants," said Morris, "and then knowing what and when to give, and what to hold on to. Also, the person you're negotiating with has to want to work with you. Much of the negotiation depends on personal relationships and also on communication. It's very important to find out what may be bothering the other person about the deal, or about you, and then initiate a discussion to deal with those issues. This provides the basis for reaching common ground. If you don't deal with the real issues now, they're going to be ten times worse down the line. The person has to like you, trust you, and want to work with you. It's an old cliché, but making a good business partnership is very much like dating that leads to a marriage. If you don't have a good relationship, there's no deal, no marriage. As long as the two of you are in the same ball park with a fair deal, and you like the guy you are working with, you go with him, because he's going to be easier to work with, especially when things get tough."

In June, the three partners had a deal, the first deal Morris had closed. The new company's name was Neose. Now we needed the start-up money, which ranged into several millions of dollars. Without the money, the company would fold. I went to work on raising the needed capital.

We raised $2 million to get the company off the ground. For the next couple of years, Neose created sugars to be used in a wide assortment of products, the first of which was baby formula. The sugars Neose produced were similar to those found in breast milk, which are far more compatible with infants' digestion. Like the sugars in breast milk, Neose's sugars could promote the development and strength of an infant's immune systems.

"It takes a long time to produce these sugars," explained Morris Laster. "We started out with a small batch and after many months, we had a much larger sample, but we didn't have enough yet to mass market our products."

Still, once Neose was up and going, word of its potential spread widely within the biotechnology industry. Soon, they were being pursued by leading bankers and venture capitalists, including Goldman Sachs, one of the world's premier investment bankers. Goldman Sachs wanted to raise money for Neose so that they could profit from the company's soon-to-be-realized potential. When Neose needed more money, Goldman Sachs tried to get $10 million for the company. Unfortunately, they failed to raise a single dollar for Neose, which was now close to bankruptcy.

At that point, Steve Roth came back to us and we agreed to represent Neose. The company needed a minimum of $10 million. Lindsay Rosenwald asked me to raise the money. The job was not going to be easy, Lindsay said. First, Goldman Sachs had already scoured the field looking for cash and failed miserably. Second, we had to have the money in eight weeks; otherwise, the company would collapse.

I came up with a strategy that included getting U.S. Healthcare, the nation's largest HMO, to invest in Neose. It seemed to me like a natural pairing. The sugars produced by Neose were going to be used in a wide variety of medical applications, including, as I said, vaccines for cancer. That had to appeal to the giant HMO.

I realized that given the limited time table we were on, I had to go directly to Len Abrahamson, the chairman of U.S. Healthcare. I soon discovered that that was not going to be so easy as it sounded. The reason: He refused to answer or return any of my 35 telephone calls, which I made over a six-week period. Finally, I was directed to Sherrill Neff, senior vice president of strategic investments for U.S. Healthcare. I told Mr.

Neff's secretary that I wanted only 30 seconds of his time. If Mr. Neff was not interested in what I had to say, I would not call again. Soon, Mr. Neff was picking up the telephone. "Go," he said, informing me with a single word that I literally had only 30 seconds to make my pitch.

"There is a company down the street from you that you will buy in five years, or they will buy you in ten. Can I continue?"

A long pause and then a single word: "Continue," he said. Now I had his attention and the chance to sell Neose, which I did. Shortly after our conversation, the principals got together and U.S. Healthcare decided to invest $2 million. The relationship between Neose and U.S. Healthcare became even deeper when, a year later, Sherrill Neff decided to become president of Neose Technologies.

Getting U.S. Healthcare on board was a big coup, but it wasn't enough. We still needed $8 million, the lion's share of which I got from International Institutional Investors and four men who were on the *Forbes* list of billionaires. One of them was the man I met in the revolving door, whom I mentioned in Chapter 1. In any case, within eight weeks, we had raised $12.6 million and Neose was on solid ground. Over the next few years, my team of investment bankers and venture capitalists would raise nearly $30 million for Neose.

KERYX: THE TOUGH ROAD BEGINS

With Neose growing steadily, Morris began to look for new frontiers to enter, which is when he discovered Dr. Ben-

Sasson's work and the creation of Keryx. We at Paramount Capital knew that Morris had another winner. Indeed, Keryx had the potential to be one of the most powerful companies in the 21st Century.

Once we had a deal worked out with the University of Pennsylvania and our scientific partners, including Dr. Shmuel Ben-Sasson and his team, we went to work to raise the money needed to create Keryx. Morris and I went to Europe and the Middle East to see investment bankers. Morris described the technology and I sold the package—a dog-and-pony presentation that is typically referred to as a "road show." One of the first investors who eagerly pursued us was a bank from England who promised to give us the $8 million needed to start the company.

The English bank liked us from the start. It didn't take much to recognize the enormous medicinal and financial potential of our products, and the $8 million we wanted for 40 percent of the company was a bargain. The important factors to us were the cash and the fact that we did not have to give up a controlling interest in the company. We'd still be in charge, which was an essential part of the deal for us.

We all agreed with the details of the deal and the bank promised to make the $8 million investment. Before they did, however, they wanted to research the market further and understand the full potential of our product line. They also wanted to better understand our strengths and weaknesses as a company.

Our glaring weakness, of course, was cash flow. We had brilliant ideas and a series of potentially history-making products, but we couldn't wait very long for the money. Without a near-term infusion of capital, we would be dead in the water. That was our vulnerability and the English bank officers saw it immediately. Be patient, they kept telling us. Let us research the market, understand the product line a little better, they said. In a short while, the $8 million will be in your account.

The English bank strung us out for four months. When they knew that we were teetering on the brink of bankruptcy, they came to us with an offer. We could be absorbed as part of one of their own weaker companies that was itself in financial trouble, or we could look elsewhere for funding. In other words, they had put us on the brink of collapse and then offered to take control of us entirely as our only option for survival. They planned to use Keryx to shore up one of their own failing companies, which was not worth saving on its own merits, apparently. With Keryx folded into their own company, they would invest heavily because they would have a product line worth supporting, one that would pay off big down the line.

We were in big trouble; there was no doubt. Our backs were against the wall. Also, after months of expecting to be partners with the English bankers, there was a subtle pressure on us to capitulate to their demands. We were already working with them, some inner voice was telling us. Why not just throw our lot in with them and see what we could salvage from the wreckage? But the way they had manipulated us was too much to swallow. These were unscrupulous people who would tear us to pieces if we allowed them to take over.

No dice, we told them. The deal was off. The bank officers were sure we would collapse in a matter of a few days, maybe a week or two at most. We didn't.

IS THAT A KNIFE IN MY BACK?

At Keryx, the CEO immediately cut expenses across the board to keep the company alive. Meanwhile, I started telephoning potential investors from all over the world to get people excited about the technology we had under development. I also set up road shows with potential investors. Morris and I were sharing rooms in little hotels in Europe and the U.S. We were desperate. Somehow, in a matter of a few weeks, we had managed to raise just enough capital to keep ourselves going for a few more months. And then the sun seemed to rise again: An Israeli bank offered to bail us out by investing $8 million.

All they needed, they said, was enough time to do their own due diligence.

After looking over our prospectus and studying the technology and the field we'd be entering, the Israeli bank loved us. Their senior officers came to us and urged us to sign a letter of intent, which spelled out our agreement and the details of the partnership we were about to enter. It was a good agreement, just what we negotiated. The only problem with it was that there was a "no shop" clause in the letter which limited the amount of money we could raise—and the number of shares we could sell—while the bank did its market and technology research. This is a fairly standard clause and is designed to protect the prospective investors from having the company sold out from under them while they do their due diligence and prepare an agreement.

But here's an important lesson that I learned the hard way during the Keryx negotiations. You never sign a "no shop" clause without the other party putting a significant amount of money at risk in case they back out at the last minute. Both parties have to have something to lose, as well as gain. I did not insist that the Israeli bankers put money on the table that they would lose if they backed out of our agreement. That was a mistake.

We signed the agreement and, in the process, tied our own hands by promising not to raise any significant amount of capital while the bank officers did their market research.

Still, on the surface, the deal was good. The bank had the money and it seemed we could do business with their officers. Meanwhile, I raised a small amount of capital to keep us going while we waited for the bank to finally deposit the funds.

A month later, we were still waiting. Three months passed and still no decision from the bank. They were clearly extending us, as the English bank did. Meanwhile, our funds were dwindling and we had to have capital. Four months passed and still no agreement—only promises. After six months, we were broke. Now the bankers came to us with a new offer: They wanted the whole company for $6 million—take it or leave it. Otherwise, the deal was off.

Morris called me at about 6 P.M. with the news. At 7 P.M., I was making telephone calls and arranging road shows all over again. Our CEO made new changes at Keryx to let us get by on a shoestring. The Israeli investment bank thought they had us by our throats. They were waiting for us to collapse and come crawling back to them for life. Like the English investors, they underestimated us badly. We would sooner sink than be controlled by unscrupulous people.

Still, the duplicity from both sets of bankers was taking its toll. I have done a lot of deals in my twenty years of business, but this one was particularly difficult. We had what we believed to be a history-making technology in our hands, and yet we were being frustrated and cheated at every turn. Sometimes you feel that your every move is blocked by obstacles, many of them put there by enemies. This was one of those times.

Morris and I were under tremendous stress and I, for one, was starting to break down. I suffered from searing headaches and backpain that periodically forced me to stay in bed for days at a time. In fact, I would eventually require back surgery to relieve the pain. I was irritable and angry—which, in truth, is rare for me. Occasionally, the anger exploded, usually on some innocent person, such as my wife. If I wasn't behaving badly, it seemed, I was apologizing for my bad behavior. It was terrible. I was strung out to my physical and emotional limits. But I learned a lot about myself and about life during that period. One of the lessons that was indelibly imprinted in my soul was that if there are delays, they are usually for a good reason. Perhaps you are trying to force a relationship with people you shouldn't be in partnership with. The truth is, I knew it on some level. Yes, the people we were dealing with were charming and outwardly courteous, but they were stabbing us in the back. How can you go into a long-term partnership with people whom you know to be unprincipled? Maybe something better is about to come along, I kept telling myself. The universe is a friendly place, I kept telling myself. Everything will work out. Stay in the saddle, hold on to your principles, and keep working for what you believe to be right.

We were barely alive, but we wouldn't be for long unless something happened. Morris and I got back on the road, desperate for a breakthrough. If we didn't get an infusion of capital soon, the company was finished.

And then a new light showed. New research was announced on a drug licensed by Keryx that showed a dramatic improvement in health for people with diabetes. Shortly after the data was published, it was presented at a large meeting for the American Diabetes Association (ADA) and was enthusiastically received. Suddenly, a company that had a valuation of $20 million a year ago was now worth $200 million.

Now I had both my belief in Keryx's technology and the scientific support that demonstrated the efficacy of one of our products. That was the moral ground on which I based my actions. Once again I was calling on investors, but this time I was armed with very convincing proof. A conversation I had with one wealthy investor characterized my approach. The man was worth nine figures and I was asking him for a minimum investment of $1 million.

"What kind of return am I going to get for my money?" he asked me.

"I can't tell you that," I said. "It's against the law to make that kind of speculation. All I can do is show you our business plan, explain the technology, the scientific data that supports our approach, and tell you how many shares of our company you will get for your money. I can also tell you about the kind of people we have working with us."

"Yes, but you can give me some idea of the kind of return I will be getting," he insisted. "You must know the kind of return you expect to have within the next few years."

"Let me ask you a question," I said. "If I get you five times the value of your investment, will it make any difference in your lifestyle?"

"No," the man admitted. "But that's not the point. I'm not in the habit of throwing my money away."

"What if I get you a tenfold return on your money. Will that change your lifestyle at all?"

"No, it won't," the man said. "But. . ."

"What if I lose your entire investment?" I asked him. "Will that affect your lifestyle?"

"No."

"Okay, but if your money gets us closer to a cure for diabetes and cancer, will that affect your life—and your children's lives?" I asked him.

"Yes, it will," he admitted.

"Well, that's the worst-case scenario," I told him. "In the worst case, I'm going to give you the most important return on your investment."

With that, he invested the one million dollars.

Within two months of the Israeli bank's attempt at a takeover, we had our $8 million and Keryx was up and running.

MORE TROUBLE, ONE MORE ESCAPE

At that point, we thought we were home free, but we still had to take the company public. In order to do that, we needed an underwriter who would raise the capital needed to do a public offering, or IPO, and a fairly stable market in which biotech stocks looked like a good investment. Both of these factors proved more difficult than we expected.

In the spring of 2000 it seemed that everybody and his brother was attempting to launch an IPO. We couldn't get any of the big underwriters to even take a meeting with us, much less get them to actually take us all the way. After a lot of turndowns, we finally got Juliet Thompson, a senior underwriter at West LB Bank, one of Europe's biggest investment banks. West LB agreed to take us public that summer. There was a lot of work to do yet. Ms. Thompson had to understand the technology involved and then raise about $40 million so that we could be publicly traded on the NASDAQ and AIM Stock exchanges. Roth Capital of California was the lead U.S. underwriter with senior bankers Lisa Walters and Jennifer Dore negotiating with Juliet. Dr. Fariba Ghodsian, Roth's biotech analyst—whom I met a decade earlier and introduced her to Avigen when it was only $7 per share—believed in Dr. Laster and Keryx's technology. Together they helped Keryx become the first company to go public simultaneously on the NASDAQ and AIM exchanges.

Meanwhile, in March 2000 the market crashed and the biotech index dropped through the floor, from 800 to 450. There was no way an underwriter would take us public if the market was bad. Investors would be scared off by a bear market, especially in biotech stocks, which would sink our IPO. Basically the bank wouldn't risk their money taking us public if they thought the market wouldn't respond positively to our offering.

I told Juliet not to worry. I predicted that in six weeks, the biotech index would be up to 525, which would be the first sign that we could launch our company in the summer. By the summer, the index would go to 650, I said.

"If that happens, Peter, we can do it," Juliet said.

In six weeks' time, the index reached 580—55 points over my prediction. By summer, the index reached 700, 50 points above what I said it would hit. People thought I had a crystal ball. Little did they know I was bluffing the whole time in order to keep people on board and to keep them moving forward.

Actually, it wasn't entirely a bluff. The Food and Drug Administration had 40 new drugs under consideration and they were prepared to release evaluations of most of them through the spring and summer. If several proved valuable, pharmaceutical and biotech stocks would get a boost, I believed. All we needed was for the FDA to go along with those drugs and the index would rise. Keryx would rise with it. As it turned out, the FDA did approve several of those drugs, the index got a boost, and Keryx made its initial offering on July 23, 2000.

Only a handful of people knew what it took to bring the company into existence.

CHAPTER 5

How to Get the Answer You Want

A pessimist sees the difficulty in every opportunity;
an optimist sees the opportunity in every difficulty.
                                    —Winston Churchill

W hen it comes to sales or negotiations, the word "no" rarely, if ever,
means "never." What it usually means is that we've just started
to get to know each other.

During the 1980s, it took, on average, one hundred business calls to get a single investor. There were a lot of rejections
before a deal was struck. Even the most successful people continue to experience rejection on their way to further success.
My two mentors, Ed O'Connor, now vice president and portfolio manager at Salomon Smith Barney, and Gary Cohen, a
national sales manager at Fidelity, taught me that being turned
down is an essential step on the path to success.

Today, whenever I want something badly enough, I never
allow anyone's negative answer to dissuade me. I've seen too
much not to realize that the path of every successful venture is
littered with "no's."

My own past is a story of overcoming the word "no," as I
am sure yours is, or will become, depending on how far into
your career you are. After I graduated from college, my first job
on Wall Street was with E. F. Hutton. I worked as a stock broker, beginning my day at 7:30 A.M. and quitting at 9 P.M. All day

long, I sold stocks, bonds, Ginny Maes, or mortgages, and unit investment trusts. You think of stockbrokers as being on the telephone all day long, but I tried to sell stocks by going door to door. I was young and I had no idea what I was doing. I had energy and a great desire to succeed—and that's about all I had when I first started out in this business. I spent much of the day hearing the word "no."

After three years as a stockbroker, I became a venture capitalist and for the next two years I sold almost nothing. My job was then what it is now: to raise money for biotech companies looking for cures for many of the world's most dangerous illnesses. The companies I try to help either need money to start their work, or to grow, or sometimes to stay alive.

I have crisscrossed the globe trying to raise capital for such businesses, but in the early days of my career I had little success. "No" and "good-bye, Mr. Kash" were the words I heard most in my early days.

Of course, there were many variations on the word "no," but they all amounted to the same thing. Once I arrived in a European capital for a meeting with bankers who had held out the promise of investing in a company that I was representing, only to be told—after I had arrived—that they were no longer interested in my company, but that they had something that they wanted me to raise money for. They needed $10 million, they said. They wanted me to be their conduit to the American market. My answer, of course, was "no."

In the venture capital industry, that kind of ruse is called a *bait and switch*. A company lures you in under the pretense that they're interested in investing with you. When you meet them, they tell you they no longer want to talk about your deal, but they have one of their own for which you might consider raising capital. It's pure duplicity and infuriating, as you might imagine. Young venture capitalists are often too inexperienced (not to mention naive) to realize early on when they're being suckered into a bait-and-switch situation—that is, until they meet with their prospective clients and realize they've been had.

This happened several times to me when I was still wet behind the ears, so to speak. I flew to Denton, Texas, once in a hurricane—a flight that was so turbulent that I thought I would lose my life—only to be informed that my prospective co-investors were no longer interested in the company I was representing. As it turned out, however, they had a company they wanted me to raise money for. One of the investors in this company, they said, was Ross Perot, a very good name to have on your side, especially when you are trying to raise a lot of money. No, thank you, I told them. I left that meeting angry, frustrated, and disheartened. I later found out that their pitch was all smoke and mirrors—there was no company, only the hope of creating one, and no one was backing them, including Mr. Perot. I kicked myself for a few weeks after that meeting. How could I be so stupid to get involved with such people?

Another time, I few into Denver in a snowstorm. When I arrived at the proposed site of our meeting, a restaurant well outside the city, no one was there. The place was empty, except for the bartender, who was about to close up. I had rented an old beat-up car from Rent-a-Wreck, which is not the smartest thing to do when you're driving in a snowstorm. But I wanted to conserve money for the company I was working with at the time. We couldn't afford to rent from Hertz. I waited about an hour, hoping my four prospective clients would show up. They never did. This was early in my career and I had made the mistake of not having their home phone numbers in case of an emergency. Eventually I realized that I had wasted four hours flying to Denver, two hours of driving to this restaurant, and all the time it would take me to get home again.

Outside the restaurant, the wind blew gusts of snow the size of garbage trucks into my face and against the car. I had a cousin who lived outside of Golden whom I had agreed to meet after my business was concluded. I got onto the highway and headed in the direction of my cousin's house, driving in white-out conditions. Soon I was lost on some two-lane road in the Rockies and then the car started to cough until it passed out. I got out of the car and looked around. If there is a cold version of Hell, this might be it, I thought. Desolate, lonely, and severe. Nothing was visible except the snow that rushed into the headlights. I walked around to the side of the road and looked up at a sign that said, "Welcome to Buffalo Bill's grave." What am I doing here, I wondered. I realized that if things didn't pick up soon, they could bury my career next to Bill over there. Eventually, I got the car started, which I took to be a sign from God. My career wasn't dead, I told myself, just stalled.

Such experiences are great teachers. Today, of course, I do not go anywhere before I do due diligence on my prospective client, which means I thoroughly research the company and parties involved. As much as possible, I want to know if the parties have the capital they say they have and that they are sincere. I also want to determine if the investors and the company I am trying to join are a good fit. I don't set off until I have laid the groundwork for success. Nor do I let my associates travel without doing the same work, first. Still, it took me a long time to learn to do such work and research. Youthful enthusiasm can cost you time and money. But in my early years, such lessons were still out there to be learned. I still had a lot of "no's" to face yet.

I made numerous trips to Japan during the first two years of my career in venture capital and didn't consummate a single deal. The Japanese have a wonderful way of using the word "yes" to mean "no." It's all in the inflection. "Yes, yes, yes," they're saying, usually with a little smile, but it doesn't take you long to realize that they're really saying, "No, no, no" as politely as they can. You know it when they say, "Yes, we have a deal." I have learned that when Japanese businesspeople tell you that, their word is their oath. The Japanese are among the most loyal businesspeople of any on Earth. They will stick with you even when times are extremely tough. They literally become your investors for life and, if you are very lucky, as close as family members.

FIRST LEARN HOW TO DEAL WITH REJECTION

There is no succeeding in business without first learning how to deal with and overcome any personal feelings you may have about rejection. At this point, I'm nearly impervious to feelings of personal rejection, mostly because I've been rejected so many times in my professional life. There are only two ways to overcome any personal sense of injury or failure after being rejected. They are:

1. **Experience a lot of rejection. It makes you stronger.**
2. **Learn, grow, and evolve from it. By evolve, I mean you must improve your ideas, presentation, and personal character if you are to succeed.**

The first thing you have to realize about business is that rejection is a badge of honor. You don't go anywhere in the business world without taking risks, exposing yourself and your ideas to criticism, and then occasionally experiencing rejection for them. This takes courage. Those who have ideas must develop their ability to present those ideas effectively and eventually lead others to success. That ability does not happen overnight, however. It takes time, experience, and maturity. For those who are willing to walk that path, it will also mean experiencing lots of "no's" along the way.

Once you have been rejected, you have a choice: You can either retreat into anonymity and join the herd, or you can continue to take risks. If you continue to take risks, you will be rejected occasionally, though if you grow from the experience those rejections will become fewer in number. Still, people will tell you "no," no matter how far along in your career you go. However, in the process of being told no, something paradoxical begins to take place: You get stronger for the experience. It actually happens in the primitive part of your being, I believe, but you begin to realize that being told "no" is not such a terrible thing. In fact, the meaning of being told "no" begins to get smaller and smaller. It stops having the same impact on you.

One of the biggest mistakes you can make when you are told "no" is to stop believing in yourself. Don't think for a minute that those who reject you know more about you than you know of yourself. Early in my career, I experienced a lot of rejection when I went for job interviews. But after a certain number of rejections, I started to see that most interviewers didn't even bother to get to know me. They were looking for a certain type and decided early in the interview that I wasn't that type. In one such interview, I realized early in the meeting that the team of interviewers was not going to hire me. Rather than feel dejected, or to attempt to curry their favor, I decided I was going to be even more myself. One of the interviewers asked me how many hours did I work a day. I said I worked from 7:30 A.M. to 9:00 P.M. He then asked incredulously, "When do you eat dinner?" At first I asked myself, "What kind of question is that?" But then I said, "Between 4:30 and 6:00 P.M."

"That doesn't make sense," one of the senior partners said to me. "Why would you leave work at 4:30 to have dinner?"

"If you don't understand why, then obviously I'm not the right person for the job," I said. With that, I started to get up from my chair.

The youngest of the interviewers stopped me and asked, "Just out of curiosity, why 4:30?"

"That's when the The Three Stooges are on," I said. "It's my time to relax."

Everyone in the room laughed out loud—they knew I was kidding—and I was offered the job on the spot. What they didn't realize as they were questioning me is that I was interviewing them while they were interviewing me. I was not sufficiently impressed, so I declined their offer.

The Japanese have a concept they call *hara,* which means vital center. All martial arts are performed from this vital center, or center of gravity, which is the place just below your navel where your physical body can achieve balance and stability. Hara is more than a physical location, however. It is the combination of physical, mental, and emotional stability. Hara is also responsible for maintaining the strength of your will and your capacity to fulfill your ambitions. The Japanese think of hara as a second brain in the body, one that controls your instincts and your ability to react in challenging situations. As you experience life and develop yourself, your center of gravity becomes stronger and more powerful. It becomes more difficult for situations or people to throw you off balance. Indeed, their "no" can no longer deflect you from your purpose. In the process, you experience yourself as stronger, more centered, and balanced. You feel as if you are taking up more space upon the Earth.

Among the keys to strengthening hara is to grow from your experiences with rejection; that means, develop your talents, and refine your abilities, presentation, and self-expression. Become better and stronger at what you do.

You cannot grow from the experience of being told "no" if you deal with it exclusively in your head, so to speak. In other words, you cannot train yourself to think in a new way and then expect to be comfortable with the word "no." It won't happen. People who think that they can change their thinking patterns without changing their behavior are doomed to a lifetime of rejection. You've got to change the way you do business. In other words, the "no" you hear has to become an incentive for growth and evolution.

When you are being told "no" on a regular basis, you cannot escape the fact that people are not responding to you in the way you would like. You've got to reflect on why they are reacting as they are and then change your behavior. Therefore, the first step in your evolution must be to determine why people say "no" to you.

One of the things I do today to strengthen my chances of success is to take a new deal first to the people I know will say "no." These people are going to ask a lot of tough questions; they will also expose many of the deal's weaknesses. I want to know those weaknesses and confront those tough questions. In a sense, the people who say "no" to me are giving me a test run; they're allowing me to practice making my pitch and to confront my weaknesses, before I go out there and deal with the people to whom I want to sell this deal.

People just starting out in their careers should do something similar: They should go to as many interviews as they can, just to understand what it takes to perform under such conditions and to practice responding to all the tough questions you're going to face.

UNDERSTAND WHY PEOPLE SAY YES OR NO

One of the things we should all want to understand is why people say "no." I believe that the first and most important reason people say "no" is because of fear. There are several possible reasons people are afraid. It's your job as the salesperson to figure out why the person is saying "no."

FIRST, BE TRUSTWORTHY

The first fear that many prospective clients experience is a fear of you. They may not trust you. People are especially distrustful of those who are aggressive and too eager to make a deal. People are especially distrustful of salespeople who are in a hurry. The faster a salesperson is moving you to make a purchase or investment—especially in the early stages of your relationship—the more it seems he's concerned only with your money. Most of us do not trust those who are too singularly focused on money. We all fear that once a salesperson has our money, he or she will abandon us, especially if something goes wrong with the product we just purchased.

We also worry that we will be cheated. When you think about it, you realize that the more superficial your relationship with a salesperson, the greater will be your fear of being cheated. Indeed, in most cases, those who sell bad products, or cheat others, want to avoid deeper relationships and personal commitments.

That means, of course, that you've got to develop a relationship with your clients that is larger than just business. One of the lessons I have learned over the years is not to meet my prospective client or do any business on the day I arrive in a city, especially if it's in a foreign country. I go to the museums or the city's latest attractions. I get a feeling for the people, the character of the city, and what's going on there, and take the pulse of the economy. I do this so that I can talk about things other than business with my prospective client. This allows me to open up the conversation so that we can get on more human ground. It gives me a chance to get to know the person with whom I am doing business. Just as I want to get to know this person, I also want him or her to get to know me. I'm not just a man doing business. I have a wife and three children and all the normal issues associated with family life. I have my hobbies and certain pastimes that I enjoy. I'm very concerned about world events and I'm a sports fan. As we all know, we bring our whole lives to our business relationships. I might as well acknowledge my larger life, and that of my client. In fact, I believe that most people with whom I do business want to feel they know me, just as much as they want to be known.

I am also a believer that people see your larger life, even when you try to hide it. If you are a person of honesty and integrity, people see and feel that. You don't have to say a single word about either; people can sense who you are. Yes, they can be wrong about you. You can be wrong about them. That's why you allow the person to get to know you, just as you want to get to know your prospective client. Soon, the information you have about each other, as well as your intuitive feelings, combine to tell you whether you will be able to do business with this person.

Another important approach, especially to a new client, is try to avoid conducting business on your first meeting or visit. I realize that sometimes people want you to get down to business immediately. Those are the easy calls, in fact. If you are developing a new relationship with a client, however, try to avoid selling him or her anything on your first call. Use the time, instead, to get a better understanding of the person, his or her business and particular needs. Let the client get sufficiently comfortable with you so that he or she can ask whatever questions may be on his or her mind. It's always better if a person buys from you, rather than you selling to him or her.

I've been doing this for the two decades that I've been in business. Naturally, many of my clients have become my friends with whom I have continued to do business. Many people avoid establishing friendships among their clients; they want to keep a professional distance from the people they do business with. I understand this practice and respect it. For me, it wasn't possible, however, for several reasons. First, my clients usually remain with me for many years. Second, I care about them and their investments. And third, I can do a better job for them if I understand their personal needs. Don't get me wrong: I do not push a relationship beyond its natural boundaries. That would be wrong. But I do want to get to know my clients as people. For me, it's natural that some of these people turn out to be friends of mine, people to whom I remain loyal.

One of the reasons I have been able to maintain these relationships is because I have tried to maintain my own integrity. By that I mean, I try to say what I know to be true, and I try to do what I say I will do. Yes, there are lots of times that you simply cannot do what you had hoped you could do within the time frame that you anticipated, but you still must do all you can to fulfill your promises, even if they take a little extra time. Above all else, people trust sincerity, which is the characteristic you develop when you commit yourself honestly and fully to any endeavor. People know it when you are doing your best, just as they know it when you aren't.

One of the best ways you can demonstrate sincerity is to call your clients immediately when things are going poorly. Don't let people find out on their own that an investment has taken a downturn. Call and let them know your thoughts, any strategies you may have come up with, and your advice on what to do now and in the long-term.

People want to trust you. In order to do that, they must feel that you see and understand them as people first. Your prospective client wants to know that you are going to take larger concerns into account when you are doing business with him or her. People want to be seen as more than a potentially lucrative account to you. In a very real sense, they want to know you care about them.

Once I attempted to get a wealthy man to invest in a business I was representing. "I will consider investing with you if you personally invest, as well, Mr. Kash."

"Why?" I asked him.

"Because if I lose my money, I want you to feel my pain," he told me.

That was a good answer, one that taught me a lot about what people want from any salesperson, especially someone who was asking for a great deal of money. In most cases, people want to know that you have also invested, or have something at risk in the deal you're trying to sell, because that tells them how much you believe in your product.

SECOND, BE KNOWLEDGEABLE

The second fear people may have of you is that they perceive that you are not sufficiently competent in your field. This is the kiss of death.

You may be a nice guy or gal, but there is no substitute for competence, knowledge, and skill. People must know that you are an expert in your field. No one will invest their money in your product, or in your ambition, if they believe you have only a superficial understanding of your job and area of expertise. There is no basis for trust and people will fairly run from you.

Interestingly, most of us will put up with a difficult personality if we know we are dealing with someone who has great skill and is an expert in his or her field. When forced to choose, we'll choose knowledge over charm every time. Why? Because charm evaporates and knowledge endures.

Part of being an expert in your field means understanding the needs and characteristics of the people in your market. I can't tell you how many enormous mistakes are made by people who know their product, but don't understand the people to whom they are selling that product.

There's an old joke about the young venture capitalist who went off to Germany to obtain investments and then came back and told his boss that he had raised $27 million from three different bankers. His boss was both pleased and impressed.

"How did you do it?" the boss asked the young businessman.

"Well, I went to three different German banks and when asked how much they wanted to invest, they all said the same thing, 'Nine, nine, nine.'"

The joke is funny in part because people can't believe that someone could make such a stupid mistake, but very large companies have made even dumber mistakes when trying to gather business in foreign countries.

When Chevrolet tried to market its Nova sedan in Spain, the car failed miserably there. Only after they had lost millions did they realize that Nova was very close to the Spanish words *no va*, which mean "no go."

An American perfume maker tried to market a fragrance in Germany with the name "Mist." The word means "manure" in German.

Ronald McDonald failed miserably as a marketing symbol in Japan because white face means death to the Japanese.

Coca-Cola tried to sell Coke in 2-liter bottles in Spain, only to find out later that very few Spanish people have refrigerators large enough to hold 2-liter bottles of Coke. Needless to say, no one bought them.

Kellogg's Pop Tarts failed in Britain because, at the time, very few households had toasters.

General Mills lost millions when they tried to sell cake mixes in Japan where approximately three percent of people had ovens.

There have been many poor translations of company slogans that resulted in disaster. Pepsi slogan, "Come alive with the Pepsi Generation," was translated in China as "Pepsi brings your ancestors back from the grave"—a very offensive pitch in a country where ancestors are revered and even worshipped.

In English, Frank Perdue's chicken slogan reads: "It takes a strong man to make a tender chicken." In Spain, the ad read: "It takes an aroused man to make a chicken affectionate."

When Parker Pens advertised their pens in Mexico, they wanted the ad to read: "It won't leak in your pocket and embarrass you." The translation, unfortunately, read: "It won't leak in your pocket and make you pregnant."

Sometimes there are very good reasons for saying "no."

THIRD, HONOR AND OWN YOUR SUCCESS

Once I was attempting to get Irving Kahn, a member of Forbes 400 who pioneered the technology that provided up-to-the-minute stock market quotes to Wall Street, to invest in a company I deeply believed in. He fairly shocked me when he said, "Mr. Kash, how much money do you have in your bank account right now?"

Without any hesitation, I said, "I don't have that much money, but you can only appreciate how much money I have, and how successful I am, if you also know how far I have come," I told him.

"That's right," Mr. Kahn said. "But you have to understand, I only want to invest money with people who have made money for themselves. How can a person make money for me if they haven't made money for themselves?"

Mr. Kahn didn't really want to know how much money I had. What he wanted to do was make a point. And as crude as his question was, I realized that he had an excellent point to make. Why would he want to invest with me if I wasn't successful myself?

When it comes to buying a product or investing in some venture, people want to associate with success. That means that they have to believe in you as a successful person. That does not mean you have to be wealthy, or live in a house you can't afford, or wear suits that are ridiculously priced. All of those symbols may be a false facade, a lie, which will eventually contribute to your fall. What you have to communicate to people is that you have the qualities that form the foundation for success—namely, trustworthiness, integrity, knowledge, and skill.

When you have these characteristics, you are a successful person. Whatever you have in the bank right now will grow, because sooner or later your achievements will increase and your financial rewards will accrue with them.

On the other hand, if you do not possess these characteristics, better hold on to what money you have, because the chances are excellent that you will make mistakes and your money will not endure.

The great sages of the past would ask their students, "Who is rich?" The students used to give all the routine answers: "He who has great wealth." "He who has a great name." "He who has a great family."

"No," the sage would say. "Who is rich? He is rich who is happy with what he has."

This cannot be accomplished, however, with some trick of the mind. You have to evolve in your behavior, said the wise men of old.

"Who is wise?" the sage would ask. After the routine answers, the sage would answer: "Who is wise? He whose deeds exceed his words. However, if his wisdom exceeds his deeds, his deeds will not endure and his words will mean nothing."

FOURTH, TRUST THE WEB OF LIFE

Even though I was being told "no" on a regular basis early in my career, I never stopped trusting that things would get better. Somehow I would get a break, I believed. Breaks often come in strange ways.

On the night I was to be engaged, I was walking down Lexington Avenue near Grand Central Station in New York City when I saw two Japanese men standing on a corner struggling over a map of the city. I went over to them and asked if they needed help. They didn't speak much English. I had had a year of Japanese and believed I could communicate very simple ideas. I asked them where they wanted to go. They gave me the address of an American steak house. I asked them if they would rather eat at a good Japanese restaurant and they said yes. I made the suggestion in part because I had hoped they could find people who spoke Japanese and English and could help them with the language. I escorted them to the restaurant, but when we got there, they insisted I eat with them.

I agreed to have a quick meal with them. A few flasks of sake later, we were laughing and getting to know each other. Fortunately, there was a waitress who spoke perfect English and Japanese and who served as our translator through most of the evening. Her name was Keiko Shioda. Young, attractive, and smart, Keiko was a wonderful translator. In the course of that evening, I asked Keiko to come to work for me as a translator. She agreed.

As it turned out, both of the gentlemen I had helped were successful businessmen in Japan. One was the president of a Japanese investment firm and the other was his secretary. The chairman of the investment firm was one of the wealthiest people in Japan. What these two men were doing on the street, as opposed to being driven to their appointment, I still don't know. In any case, thanks to Keiko, we all realized that we shared many business interests and believed we might be able to join in a business venture. I was eager to make contacts in Japan and to finally consummate a deal there, after having failed many times before. I thought that this might be my golden opportunity. It wasn't. Shortly after we met, a possible business arrangement with my new Japanese friends fell through, but they introduced me to another Japanese businessman with whom I struck my first successful transaction in Japan. Keiko was my translator.

It was a multimillion-dollar investment by Japanese bankers for a biotech firm that I represented. The arrangement seemed charmed. The investors were perfect for the company and all the principles seemed to get along perfectly—that is, until one little word in the contract nearly blew everything out of the water. The word was "it."

The "it" in question referred to the company's name, but the Japanese believed it to mean another party to the agreement. "Who is 'it'?" they wanted to know. "What is 'it' doing as part of this agreement?" Unfortunately, it took us days to even understand what the real complaint was. All we knew for the longest time was that there was a problem with the contract, which the Japanese would eventually get around to telling us. Only after several hours on the phone at 3 A.M.—there's a 14-hour difference between Tokyo and New York—did we finally come to realize that the word "it" was the issue, and why "it" was a problem at all.

It was Keiko who finally broke through for us at a point when it seemed that everything might break down. She came to me privately and explained the problem. Apparently, the Japanese wanted to use their own translator—they would not use Keiko. The Japanese translator was having problems making sense of the word "it."

Once the problem became clear, we were able to dispense with it fairly easily, but I realized something very important in the process: Small things can disrupt communication and turn "yes" into "no" very easily.

RECOGNIZING THE POWER OF
SOMEONE WHO CAN SAY NO

Only people in a position of power and authority can say "no." Even if the person is running the stock room and is in a position to say "no" to your product, he or she has the authority to make such a decision. Once you find a person who can say "no," you have found a center of authority. With the right influence, a person who says "no" can sometimes be persuaded to say "yes."

When I first started out in business, I spent most of my time on the people who said "yes" and those who said "maybe." I spent almost no time with those who said "no." That was a mistake. People who say "maybe" are usually a waste of time. They can't make a decision and many of them are just hoping you will go away. Those who say "no," however, should be reviewed and reflected upon and very often gone back to. I want to know why they said "no," what their concerns were. Sometimes I tell a person, "If I can convince you that I can relieve you of your concerns, do I have a chance to persuade you to say yes?"

Many of them do.

In 1989, I read an article in the *New York Times* about a new fund with $5 million in capital, called the Kaufman fund, which was managed by a very astute businessman by the name of Hans Utsch. Mr. Utsch was looking for small growth companies to invest in and I had such a company that I believed was a perfect match for his fund. I called Mr. Utsch, got his secretary, and was quickly rebuffed. Mr. Utsch was busy, she said. So I called his office nine more times that day until I finally got through to him. On my tenth attempt, Mr. Utsch picked up the phone and asked me what I wanted.

I told him that I had seen the article in the *Times* and had a company that I thought would be ideal for his fund. I described the company, gave its name, and said that the CEO would be in my office at 5 P.M. the next day. Did he want to attend? Yes, he said, and with that he abruptly hung up.

I was so stunned by the suddenness of it all that I was too embarrassed to call him back and ask if he knew where my office was located. The next day, he arrived at my office on time, having thoroughly researched the company. After listening to the CEO, Mr. Utsch invested $100,000. Two years later, he sold at eight times his original investment.

The Kaufman Fund is one of the most successful mutual funds with assests of more than $6 billion.

As my mentors, Ed O'Connor and Gary Cohen, used to tell me: When you hear the word "no," realize that you are that much closer to making a deal, because mathematically you have just eliminated one more "no" on the way to "yes." In reality, negotiations don't start until you hear the word "no." Then you're talking to someone who has authority and is in a position to say "yes." That's when the game begins.

CHAPTER 6

When to Make a Leap of Faith and When to Walk Away

The best way to have a good idea is
to have lots of ideas
—Linus Pauling

*O*pportunities are paradoxical gifts. The only way you can obtain their rewards is to put something valuable at risk. Though we typically don't think of it in these terms, every opportunity, in fact, is a chance to gamble. That's the way the game of life is played. Allow me to give you an example.

As I have said earlier in this book, I went to Japan for more than two years without closing a single deal. It wasn't for lack of trying. I had made numerous trips to Tokyo already and had even offered some very good deals to the Japanese. Two of the companies I had tried to get Japanese firms to invest in—Summit Technology and Marrow Tech—had gone up several-fold. My problem, in part, was that I was young. Although my title was Senior Vice President, I was only 28 years old and looked more like 20. The Japanese people—especially their businessmen—respect experience and age and I had little of either. Still, I kept trying.

In February 1990, I was back in Tokyo to meet the President of Yamaichi Univen, the venture capital subsidiary of Yamaichi Bank, the fourth largest bank in the world. I was in Tokyo to get Yamaichi and other Japanese firms to invest in

Interneuron Pharmaceuticals, Inc., for which I was attempting to raise start-up capital. Very few Japanese investment houses had funded an American biotech IPO, and Yamaichi was not among those that had. I would also meet six other firms and then travel to Hong Kong to seek out other possible investors.

After an eighteen-hour flight to Tokyo, via Hong Kong, and a two-hour bus ride to the Imperial Hotel in downtown Tokyo, I arrived in late afternoon. I unpacked my bags and found a note from my fiancée. The note said, "Don't worry about business. Just be yourself and have fun." I fell asleep that afternoon and awoke at 7:30 the next morning. An hour later, I was on the famed Moarnochi Red Line to Yamaichi headquarters.

For six months, I had pitched Interneuron to Yamaichi. Fortunately the technology that supported Interneuron was created by M.I.T., which held some weight with the Japanese. Blue-chip names are important when selling overseas. At Yamaichi, I pitched Interneuron to six of Yamaichi's top executives, including the firm's president Mr. Shinozaki. The presentation took two hours. During that time, I somehow managed to befriend my interpreter, who slyly advised me when to speak and when to keep quiet. Once I had concluded, the president and his team suggested that we meet for dinner that night.

At 6:30 P.M. I met my hosts at a French restaurant and thus began a long evening of drinking and eating, with heavy emphasis on the former. A great banquet of food was paraded out before us. Just as great were the quantities of alcohol. We started out with Suntory beer and then followed the customary trend to sake, Scotch, and cognac. After much talk and increasing laughter, the bill finally arrived. Holding to form, several junior executives offered to pay, but in Japan even the paying of the bill is subject to sacred tradition. That right falls to the senior person at the table, in this case the company president, Mr. Shinozaki.

"No, no," I said. "I have learned so much from this experience that I would like to pay." I hadn't even looked at the bill at that point. Mr. Shinozaki gave me a sly smile and said, "Dijobo Des," meaning "Okay." Without hesitation I placed my American Express card on the table. It was then that I looked at the bill: $7,500! Yikes! I thought. My cedit limit is $5,000. Suddenly, the entire table started laughing. Did they know my credit limit was $2,000 below the cost of the bill? "He's only joking," one of the junior people said about Mr. Shinozaki's comment. The president would pay the bill. I revealed no hint of relief. "Okay," I said reluctantly. "I bow to tradition." The president gave me a conspiratorial smile, with a hint of fondness in his eyes. Maybe he knew, but that didn't matter. My credibility had just gone up.

We moved to the piano bar where more drinks were served. I was trying desperately to hold on to the little bit of sobriety I had left. It wasn't easy. The only thing that convinced me that I wasn't entirely drunk was that I still knew why I was there: I meant to consummate a deal with the president of Yamaichi that night. How was I going to do that, I kept wondering. The more people drank, the more bawdy the stories and jokes became. Any thought of business was essentially in the next galaxy—a galaxy that, thanks to the Scotch, seemed far, far away. Finally, inspiration struck me. Do I dare? I wondered. I'm pretty drunk, I thought, and I haven't done that trick since college. What if I fail? Yamaichi was my best hope for an investor on this trip. What would I say to the

Interneuron executives if I blew this possibility? They were counting on me. Suddenly, I remembered Donna's note: "Just be yourself and have fun," it said.

I asked the bartender for a deck of cards. He reached below the cash register and handed one to me.

"Shinozaki-san," I said. "I am going to let you pick any card from this deck. You look at the card and then place it back in the deck. I'm going to shuffle the cards and then place the deck in front of us. If I pick your card, your firm will give me a $1 million investment for Interneuron. If I fail to pick your card, I go home without the investment, and without any hard feelings. Is it a deal?"

He paused and then gave me a big smile. He liked to play for big stakes, too. "Hai," he said. In that instant, I knew that I had just closed my first deal in Japan.

I held out the deck and Shinozaki-san picked a card. "Okay," I said, "look at your card and then put it back in the deck without showing it to me." He complied.

I shuffled the deck extensively and then placed it on the table in front of the president. I asked him to tap the deck three times and then turn over the top card. It was the card he had chosen. "Shingin Nariui!" he cried, which meant, "Unbelievable!"

The million dollars was wired to my firm before I returned to New York. Yamaichi Univen sold three years later and made eight times on their money.

MAKING THE LEAP

The details of each golden opportunity are as different as each of us, but they all boil down to the same kinds of situations.

Suddenly, you have a chance to put together a deal that will change your career; or a project drops in your lap whose success could set your career on a whole new path; or you have the chance to open your own business. Saying "yes" to your golden opportunity will suddenly place enormous responsibility on your shoulders. You very likely will have to cope with additional stress and strain. As we all know, success is never guaranteed. You've jumped and failed before—we all have, at one time or another. If you fail, you'll get the blame. If you succeed, you'll get the rewards. Either way, your life will be changed dramatically.

What do you do?

A lot depends on who you are. Most people, I believe, tend to emphasize only one side of opportunity and de-emphasize the other. Some see opportunity largely as a chance to realize a goal. They may say that they see the potential pitfalls implicit in the situation, but they're so excited by the possible rewards that they de-emphasize the risks. Unfortunately, many of these people leap before they look, because they're either greedy or naive. People who jump into situations where even "angels fear to tread" get burned repeatedly until they become wise or bitter.

Some years ago, I was given the great honor of having dinner with the former Prime Minister of England, Margaret Thatcher. There were about six of us at the table, including Mrs. Thatcher and me. At one point in the conversation, I seized the opportunity to launch off into a lengthy presentation about recent medical advances in biotechnology. The truth is, I was showing off, and in this case, I had leapt before I looked. After I concluded my remarks, Mrs. Thatcher gave her own presentation about biotech, which was far more impressive than mine.

With more than a little humility, I said, "Lady Thatcher, how did you gain such a sophisticated knowledge of biotechnology and medicine?"

In her most aristocratic tone, Mrs. Thatcher replied, "Mr. Kash, obviously, you haven't read my book. Otherwise, you would have known that I am a chemist by training."

I felt like I had just been slam-dunked. And to this day, the image I have of her in that moment is that she is looking down at me from a great height. One of the lessons I derive from such situations is that there's a big difference between making a leap because your livelihood depends on it—and because the circumstances support it—and making one because your ego is temporarily inflated.

It's important to make such distinctions—that is, between the heart and the ego—because if you get slam-dunked enough, you can start to see opportunities as dangerous situations that very likely will result in failure and loss. Those who see life in those terms run the risk of withdrawing even when they are looking at the chance of a lifetime. Unfortunately, there is only so much retreating you can do before you yourself get smaller and smaller and end up living, as Henry David Thoreau said, a life of quiet desperation.

How you behave in the face of an opportunity oftentimes depends on how you see life; or, to invoke Einstein's famous question, whether or not you see the universe as a friendly place. Interestingly, those who say that the universe is not a friendly place not only avoid jumping at their golden chance, but very often are unable even to recognize it when it shows up.

Many times I have offered wealthy investors deals that had success written all over them. Yet, they decided against taking the risk, which soon proved to be the wrong decision.

My point is that we all must learn when to leap into the unknown and take that fateful risk, and when to hold back and play it safe. This is a difficult choice. Short of being a psychic, there is no way to foretell the future. Therefore, the question naturally arises: How can I decide whether or not this opportunity is right for me?

In business, there are clear guidelines for making important decisions, especially when determining whether or not to take up some new opportunity. Many tangible factors can be examined to help determine whether a company will invest in a new product, or line of products, for example, or make an acquisition. But in life—which is to say, in your career—such decisions can be more complex, in part because they are based on more amorphous factors, such as your talents, ambitions, and whether or not you are ready for such a challenge.

In this chapter, I'm going to provide you with some guidance for deciding when to make that fateful leap into the unknown, and when to refrain from leaping.

RULES FOR JUMPING

Just as with a business decision, we can develop guidelines for making career and life decisions. There may be many important factors, but I have identified seven of them which I believe will help you to determine if an opportunity being offered is right for you. When facing an important opportunity, or challenge, that you are not sure whether or not to embrace, answer the following seven questions. Then you'll know if you have what it takes to succeed in the face of that opportunity. The seven questions are as follows:

1. **WHAT IS BEING OFFERED IN THE OPPORTUNITY?** You must be very clear about what the real benefits are. Analyze the situation and ask questions to be sure that you are not fooling yourself about what really is being offered, versus what you may believe is being presented to you. Ask questions of those who are offering you this opportunity. See it for what it really is.

2. **WHAT EXACTLY DO YOU STAND TO LOSE IF THINGS DO NOT WORK OUT?** Is it money, status, a position within your company, your own business, or some other valuable resource or commodity?

3. **DO YOU HAVE ANOTHER CHOICE?** Invariably, the web of life offers us opportunities when we desperately need them. Sometimes the stress of the moment prevents us from recognizing just how good the opportunity is, but with a little reflection, and the recognition that we have few other choices, we may yet see that this is a great gift being offered.

4. **ARE YOU WILLING TO COMMIT YOUR TIME, ENERGY, AND COURAGE TO THIS ENDEAVOR?** A related important question is this: Is fear alone keeping you from going forward? Fear of failure can cause us to be tentative, insecure, and indecisive, characteristics that almost always precipitate failure. Ask yourself honestly if it is only fear that is keeping you from seeing just how good this opportunity is.

5. **DO YOU HAVE THE MATURITY, OR WISDOM, TO BEHAVE SKILLFULLY ONCE YOU ARE IN THE SITUATION?** Sometimes we

face the misfortune of having an opportunity for which we are not ready. We may not be far enough along in our career to handle such a situation. We may not have the skills as yet to cope with all the challenges such an opportunity will bring. Wisdom requires us to be honest with ourselves and to know that we should wait. Never forget the old Peter Principle, which states that people are promoted to the level of their incompetence. I believe that the Peter Principle occurs most often for people who are promoted prematurely. They may be very talented and perhaps overly ambitious. They didn't realize that excessive ambition can cause us to reach for more than we are ready to handle.

6. DOES THIS SITUATION GIVE YOU THE OPPORTUNITY TO DO SOMETHING THAT YOU ENJOY, OR EVEN LOVE? Is it part of who you are or would it require you to do things that are outside your area of interest or expertise?

7. WHAT DOES YOUR GUT TELL YOU? Without a doubt, this is the most important question of all. If something inside you resonates with joy, excitement, and courage; if your very cells are jumping to say "yes," then these feelings are enough to say "yes." Each of us possesses a kind of spiritual tuning fork inside of us, I believe. When an opportunity arises that is not right for us, something deep inside of us lets us know. A feeling emerges, a kind of dissonance that we experience as a resistance to movement. That's the tuning fork letting us know that the answer is no; hold back; wait. But when you are confronted with a great opportunity that lifts your spirit and causes something deep inside of you to leap, then you have no other choice but to follow your instinct.

Once you have asked and answered these seven questions, you should have a clear idea of the opportunity at hand and what you feel about it. The more you are on the lookout for opportunities, the better you become at recognizing them and knowing when to leap, and when to defer.

If you know what you are being offered, and it is something you love, and you know you are ready, and your gut tells you that this opportunity is right for you, then you must seize the moment and jump. To turn back in fear is to risk losing more than just a golden chance. Whether or not you realize it, something of your soul is at stake.

TO BE OR NOT TO BE . . .
THE HEROIC VERSION OF YOURSELF

What does opportunity really offer us? Is it just a better job, or an exciting project, or a business we want to open on our own? If it isn't, then what more is being offered? That more is the chance to experience the heroic version of who you are. If we habitually back away from opportunity, we find ourselves shrinking in our own eyes—and sometimes in the eyes of those who love us.

Many times I have asked myself: Why is this the case? I think the answer is that we are all blessed and cursed with a heroic image of ourselves that we long to fulfill and become. What I mean is that we have some vague, yet power picture of who we would like to be. That heroic image is different for everyone. One person longs to be a doctor, a nurse, or some form of healer; another person wants to be a great architect;

and still another, a great scientist. Some people want to be entrepreneurs; others want to be great salespeople, writers, teachers, artists, singers, dancers, film makers, bankers, mothers, fathers, homemakers, builders, business people, priests, rabbis, and ministers. You name it and someone wants to be their own idealized version of that activity or profession.

One of the difficult aspects of this dream is that it is multidimensional—meaning it includes many aspects of your life, not just your profession. To varying degrees, it contains other aspects of your life, such as your role as a parent, husband or wife, provider, and friend. But usually, there is one aspect of this dream that dominates all others and that is what we wish to become.

I say that we are "blessed" and "cursed" by the presence of this heroic image because it cuts both ways. It can lead you to become a truly fulfilled and happy person, or it can be the basis for your greatest disappointment.

The irony is that people do not have to fulfill the image entirely. In fact, every truly mature and fulfilled person that I know feels that he or she has failed to fully realize his or her heroic archetype. What mattered in the end was whether or not they went for it—that is, whether or not they gave themselves to the realization of their dream. One very wise man once told me that he failed to achieve his ambitions in every aspect of his life; even so, he saw his life as successful because he truly believed he did his best. And indeed, this man is highly successful by anyone's standard.

Another interesting thing about our heroic ideal is that no one can judge how close, or how far away, we have come to realizing that dream but ourselves. In the end, the only judgment that really matters is yours. Still, your judgment of yourself will be assessed, in part, by whether or not you leaped when the web of life offered you an opportunity. Did you jump, or did you shrink from the possibilities because you were afraid? That's the question we all will be asking ourselves at the end of the day.

I sometimes ask myself, what determines whether or not I should jump? Many times I have jumped and utterly failed— not because I was particularly unwise after I had made a commitment. I failed because I committed myself when I should have said "no." Yet, how can you know the difference between an opportunity for which you should take a risk and one that wisdom dictates should be avoided?

It's not an easy question, but it is one that we all must answer in our own ways. I answer in this way: If an opportunity comes that permits me to be more of who I long to be— that is, it gives me an opportunity to be the person I really want to be—then I jump. I take the risk and give all I can to realizing my ambition. But if an opportunity comes that I feel I am unsuited for, or is not part of my own heroic ideal, then I defer, because it will naturally lead me away from who I truly am, and long to be. In the latter case, I feel no loss at saying "no." On the contrary, I feel good that I didn't burden myself with a task or project for which I am naturally unsuited. Oftentimes, I refer the person who is making me such an offer to someone else I know who is better suited for the project.

On the other hand, when an opportunity comes that I believe is right for me—or even one that I believe will be fun and worth the risk—I jump. Something in the opportunity feels right for me. There is a strange pull that the opportunity has on me; you might even refer to it as a calling. That pull always seems consistent with something very fundamental to me and my nature. You might say that the opportunity is consistent with the things that I love and enjoy being a part of.

SOMETIMES YOU ARE
FORCED TO LEAP

One of the most consistent characteristics I have found about the web of life is that it offers great opportunities when we need them most. For that reason, it's important to stay open and attuned when opportunities present themselves during times of crisis.

Early in my career, I was hired as an investment banker with the responsibility of raising funds for biotechnology. Shortly after I was hired, a more senior member of the firm, who felt threatened by my innovative approach to business, succeeded in having me fired. The day before the deed was to be done, a secretary told me I would be let go the following day. I decided to move fast. I went to another managing partner in the firm and asked him for a job. He agreed to hire me, but only if I could come up with a deal within the next 48 hours. What was I going to do? I wasn't sure where to begin, but I was confident I could come up with something.

The following day, as expected, my employer fired me. I was still employed, thanks to my temporary agreement with the other managing partner, but the clock was ticking. Later that day, my old mentor, Herb Silverberg, called me. Herb, who had been my teacher when I was seven, had heard that I had just been working on Wall Street and wanted to know if I knew anything about private prisons. A friend of his wanted to close a deal with Correction Corporation of America, a public company dealing with private prisons, and asked Herb if he knew anyone who could help him. I had not been in touch with Herb for years, but when his friend asked him if he knew someone on Wall Street, he thought of me. Now he asked me if I could be of service to his friend. I could have backed away at that moment, admitting that I knew nothing about private prisons, or any other kind for that matter. But I was in a desperate moment in my career. I was about to be without a job unless I came up with a deal. This was the deal that the web of life was offering me. Yes, I said to Herb. I can help you.

I spent the rest of the day setting up meetings with the parties and then called the senior partner who had hired me, just as my 48 hours were about to expire. Can you attend the meeting on Monday with one of the parties? I asked. Yes, he said, though he admitted he knew nothing about private prisons, either.

That weekend, I spent $1,500 on computer time at Prudential-Bache's Library in order to learn all I could about the subject. On Monday morning, at 8:30, our potential clients arrived at our offices. Before any discussions about potential investments could begin, they wanted to know what we knew about this enterprise. With that, I launched into an hour-long presentation about the subject of private prisons, after which the clients hired us on the spot. After a second meeting that included the Correction Corporation, the clients gave us a $10,000 bonus. More important to me, I now had a job.

WHEN YOUR HEART LEAPS,
LET YOUR BODY FOLLOW

I remember the wonderful story of Debbi Fields, who loved to bake really good chocolate chip cookies. Her cookies had two distinct qualities that were different from other cookies. First, they were larger than the ordinary chocolate chip cookie. Bigger cookies. She had created a larger chocolate chip cookie so that she would eat fewer of them, which meant that she wouldn't gain weight. Second, they were soft. Up until that time, the normal chocolate chip cookie was crispy.

For years, she made cookies for her relatives, neighbors, and friends, and all agreed that no one could make cookies like Debbi. In 1977, Debbi decided that she wanted to open a little shop in her hometown of Palo Alto, California, where she intended to sell her cookies. The stimulus behind the idea was a simple need. "I needed to share something of myself with the world," she wrote in her autobiography, *One Smart Cookie* (Simon and Schuster). "I wanted to give, to be part of things. I just wasn't ready to become invisible a nonparticipant. And what I happened to have available for giving was a pretty darn good chocolate chip cookie. So, to me, selling cookies in a store was a good idea."

Unfortunately, everyone else she shared her ambition with thought a cookie store was a really dumb idea. Debbi's husband, Randy, was an economist who regularly invited his business clients—executives from major industries—home to discuss investments. Debbi would bake cookies for the people who attended these meetings. The executives uniformly loved her cookies. They loved them so much, in fact, that Debbi decided to ask their advice on opening up a cookie store.

"'What would you think about my starting a business to sell these cookies to the public?'" she asked the executives.

"'Bad idea,' they said, their mouths full of cookies. . . 'Never work. Forget it.'"

"All the professionals were negative and it made me crazy," Debbi wrote in her autobiography. "I couldn't understand it. I knew I wasn't sophisticated but I had eyes to see with. It was like they were telling me one thing yet showing me something completely opposite. It didn't make any sense at all."

Debbi asked her mother what she thought. Her mother's reply: "I cannot believe you're going to waste your life standing over a hot oven."

She asked her husband, Randy, for his advice: "Debbi, it'll never work," he said.

Debbi asked one of her longest and best friends what she thought. "Debbi, I can't imagine it ever working."

When she got people to explain why they felt it was such a bad idea, they made a long list. America wants a crispy chocolate chip cookie, not a big soft one, they said. Besides, Debbi was only 20 years old. She had no money, no job experience, and no formal business education. What could she possibly know about creating a successful business?

Remarkably, despite every authority figure telling her that her idea was crazy, she decided to pursue it. She had no money, so she decided to go to banks. Of course, every banker she shared her idea with thought it was really dumb. That is, every banker but one. A loan officer by the name of Ed Sullivan at the Bank of America decided to take a chance on Debbi. His reason: He trusted Debbi and Randy and he liked her cookies.

Ed Sullivan offered Debbi the loan, which was the moment of truth: She could launch her idea, betting everything she had on herself and her cookie recipe, or she could back away, knowing full well that every business expert to whom she had spoken—every expert but one, that is—advised her that a cookie store would fail.

On August 18, 1977, Debbi opened Mrs. Fields Chocolate Chippery. On the day she opened her doors for business, not a single customer came into the shop. Desperate, Debbi closed her doors and took her cookies out on the street, where she gave out free samples to passersby. She believed that if people just tasted her cookies, they'd be hooked on them. She was right. Soon people started following her back to her shop. On the first day, she sold $75 worth of cookies.

Of course, Mrs. Fields Chocolate Chippery went on to become one of the great successes of the 1980s. The store itself became so successful that Debbi Fields started franchising the business. Soon she had three stores in the Palo Alto area and then 15. Eventually, those 15 stores turned into 600 stores all over America and in ten other countries around the world. Eventually, Debbi would own a thousand stores. Her little cookie business would be worth more than $100 million. Eventually, Mrs. Fields Chocolate Chippery became too big for Debbi to manage and she was forced to sell it. But before she did, she wrote a series of books, beginning with a cookbook, *Mrs. Fields Cookie Book,* which sold more than 1.5 million copies and was the first cookbook ever to be on *The New York Times* bestsellers list. She did a successful PBS series and hosted her own television show, "The Dessert Show." And all of it came from her love for baking cookies and a deep faith in her own abilities.

* * *

Dineha Mohager had a similar experience. She took a seem-ingly humble pastime, a joy for creatively painting her nails, and turned it into a multimillion-dollar enterprise. Dineh enjoyed mixing nail polish to create bright designs that matched her shoes.

One day, Dineh, a 21-year-old-student at the University of Southern California, was walking through a local shopping mall. While in the mall, she was approached by a woman who asked where she might purchase the beautiful nail polish Dineh was wearing. "Oh, I made it myself," Dineh told her.

"You mean I can't buy it?" the woman asked.

"No, I'm the only one who makes it," Dineh told her sym-pathetically. This same scenario repeated itself several times that day, until Dineh realized that she made something that people wanted. Together with her sister, Pooneh, and a friend, Benjamin Einstein, Dineh created Hard Candy, a producer of exotic nail polish that a year later took in $10 million in sales.

* * *

The moral of both of these stories is never underestimate the things you are good at, nor the things that give you pleasure. Very often, there's gold in those pastimes—and a lifetime of pleasure.

TO BECOME WHAT YOU ALWAYS LONGED TO BE

After Nathan Pritikin cured himself of heart disease, he wanted to find a way to help others. He had been a successful inventor and electronics manufacturer his entire adult life, but now he believed that he had discovered something that could help thousands of people suffering from many forms of degenerative disease, including heart disease, high blood pressure, and adult-onset diabetes. After more than twenty years of intensive study, Pritikin had become an expert in these and many other medical and scientific areas. He was also fluent in the medical language. What he needed, he realized, was a scientific study that showed how effective his program was against these very illnesses.

With the help of John Kern, M.D., who was the medical director at the Long Beach California Veteran's Hospital, Pritikin gathered a group of severely ill men who were on complete disability from the Veterans Administration. All of the men had proven and extensive coronary heart disease. Some were so ill, in fact, that they weren't far from death. On January 5, 1975, Pritikin gathered up his volunteers and placed them on his diet and exercising program. The exercise regimen consisted of two to three 15-minute walks, two or three times a day, as each could manage. They were to extend their distances as their health improved. They received no other form of treatment.

When the study was finished, the group of veterans showed remarkable improvement—so much so that many of the men experienced what could only be described as a miraculous rebirth of their health.

There was more. Pritikin had a couple of patients among his veterans' group whom he believed had experienced a reversal of their coronary artery disease. Pritikin based his belief on before-and-after angiograms, a medical test that shows the extent of the cholesterol plaque clogging the arteries to the heart. After being on Pritikin's program for one year, the angiograms showed a distinct reduction in the plaques that were clogging the coronary arteries. This had never been done before. In fact, no one had even tried such a thing in humans, though it had been shown in monkeys. Pritikin, a layman, had attempted and now claimed to have accomplished reversal of coronary heart disease, something the scientific and medical establishment didn't believe was possible. Most medical doctors and scientists still did not believe that dietary fat and cholesterol had anything to do with heart disease, much less that diet could be used to cure it. Needless to say, Pritikin's statement was revolutionary and sent the medical community into an uproar.

By some stroke of good fortune (credit the web of life) Nathan was invited to a conference on heart disease in Atlanta where he reported his Long Beach Veterans' study and publicly announced his findings, along with his claim that his diet and exercise could restore people with coronary artery disease to good health. As fortune would have it, an Associated Press reporter was attending the conference and wrote a story about Pritikin's program and his study results. The story made front-page headlines around the country.

Pritikin was inundated with thousands of letters requesting more information about his program and the whereabouts of any clinic that offered his diet and exercise regimen to sick people. In fact, there was no such clinic in existence. Nor was there any program even resembling Pritikin's being offered anywhere in the world.

Nathan realized that fate was now at hand. If there was ever an opportune moment to open a health clinic that would treat seriously ill people with his program, this was it. Yet, the dangers were astronomical. If he was wrong, people would die and he would be ruined. His name would be synonymous with tragedy and scandal. He was 60 years old. By every standard of measure, he had achieved tremendous success. He owned a beautiful, sprawling home on a five-acre estate in Santa Barbara, California. He and his wife, Ilene, with whom he had been happily married for more than 30 years, had five healthy, adult children. His electronics factory in Santa Barbara was thriving. All he had to do was coast for the rest of his life and he would be remembered as a brilliant inventor, a successful businessman, a loving husband, and a good father. He knew that if he opened the clinic that he had envisioned, he was putting his entire life on the line.

Yet, he recognized that the potential to help people was even greater than the loss he might experience.

"If I wait for the medical community [to get around to offering such a program]," Pritikin recalled years later, "it will be 200 years. I better do it myself. In a week's time, I made up my mind."

Nathan got a local Howard Johnson's hotel to provide him with rooms and a kitchen. He then signed on his nephew, who was a medical doctor, to act as the medical director of what Nathan would call the Pritikin Longevity Center. His nephew knew little about nutrition and even less about what his uncle was up to, but when Nathan explained it to him, he decided to go along.

As it turned out, Pritikin's Longevity Center became one of the most successful, and most effective, programs ever created for the treatment of heart disease, high blood pressure, angina (chest pain), adult-onset diabetes, and many other serious illnesses. Objective university scientists have studied the program for the past 20 years and documented the fact that the program has saved the lives of tens of thousands of people. Pritikin single-handedly changed the way these and other illnesses are treated by medicine today.

The beauty of his decision to leap into the unknown is not just his courage—which was enormous of itself—but the fact that he had prepared himself for so many years before the web of life gave him the perfect opportunity to become the man he always longed to be. He knew he was ready when his golden chance came and he seized it. Many thousands of people are better off today because he did.

SOMETIMES YOU LEAP FOR THE FUN OF IT

Taking a risk when there is little downside actually makes life fun and more enjoyable. It's the little adventures that add to our heroic image of ourselves and make us feel better about who we are. These are no small blessings, even when they are only small adventures.

In the spring of 1995, my chairman, Dr. Lindsay Rosenwald, was invited to a special dinner for the Simon Weisenthal Holocaust Foundation where Arnold Schwarzenegger was to be the keynote speaker. Arnold was being honored for having raised millions of dollars for organizations, such as the Simon Weisenthal Foundation, that attempt to assist holocaust survivors and bring the perpetrators of the holocaust to justice.

Dr. Rosenwald invited me and eight other members of our company to attend the dinner, which cost $10,000 per table. (Lindsay very graciously covered the cost.) Prior to the dinner, a private cocktail hour with Arnold was to be held upstairs in the hotel. That gathering cost $25,000 a head and only Lindsay was attending. When the time came for the cocktail hour to begin, those attending the gathering were asked to go to the elevators and make their way up to a special room where they would personally meet Arnold. Lindsay got up and went to the elevator. Much to his surprise, I got up and went with him.

"What are you doing?" Lindsay asked me.

"Shhh," I said. "Follow my lead."

When we reached the appropriate floor, we all got out of the elevator and walked to a desk that was set up in the hall to check names and grant entrance into the room. A large security guard stood next to the man who checked each person's name. Lindsay went to the desk, gave his name, and was admitted past the security guard. I followed behind him. Instantly, the security agent grabbed the lapel of my jacket and told me to stop. With my right hand, I grabbed the security guard's hand, bent back his thumb, and forced him to release me. At the same time, I opened my jacket just a little with my left hand, a gesture that was meant to indicate that there was a gun inside my coat. "Private security," I told the guard. He looked at me, hesitated for just an instant, and then nodded me into the room. I trailed after Lindsay, whose eyes were as large as golf balls. Once inside the room, and out of sight of the guard, Lindsay and I burst into laughter.

Suddenly, Arnold came into the room and filled it with his celebrity aura. Everyone in the room immediately hurried over to him. A circular throng had gathered around him. There's no point in my going over there now, I thought. The crowd's so big, no one's going to get close to Arnold. I stayed back. Suddenly, and very quietly, a pregnant Maria Shriver entered the room. Unlike her husband's arrival, Maria entered with an unassuming countenance, as if she were trying to sneak in under the radar and avoid the crush that her own celebrity might trigger. In fact, no one noticed her. I went over to her and introduced myself. I told her that I admired what she and her family had done with Special Olympics. With that I launched into some of the groundbreaking work being done by biotech scientists for people with various mental and physical disabilities.

She was aware of a lot of this work and we engaged in a spirited discussion about exciting new treatments for handicapped people. As we talked, I noticed Arnold looking over at us from time to time. He was more than a little curious, it seemed.

Soon he was standing in front of me, a huge presence and not a little intimidating, I must say. Arnold affectionately rubbed Maria's pregnant tummy for a moment and then turned to me.

"And who are you?" he asked, his voice and accent unmistakable.

"Arnold, this is Peter Kash," Maria said. "He's in biotechnology. He finances research."

"It's a great pleasure to meet you, Arnold," I said. We shook hands. Needless to say, Arnold has a very firm grip.

Interestingly, Arnold asked me if I knew anything about organ transplantation and the risks involved. We discussed the issues of hyperacute rejection and other risks associated with transplant. Months later, Arnold had a heart valve transplant.

After he and I finished talking, I asked him if he would pose with me for a photograph. "My kids will love it," I said. He was very gracious and we took a wonderful picture together that today sits on the bookcase in my office.

Shortly after the photograph was mounted, I had my children up to my office and showed them the picture. I had not mentioned meeting Arnold Schwarzenegger before this because I wanted it to be a surprise.

When my kids saw the picture, they screamed out, "Daddy knows Turbo Man."

I had forgotten that I had taken them to the movie *"Jingle All the Way,"* in which Arnold starred as a dad trying to get his children presents at Christmas. For my kids, this was not Arnold Schwarzenegger—that man didn't even exist for them—but Turbo Man, the hero in the movie.

"That's right," I said. "I met Turbo Man. And he's a very nice man."

* * *

We all must be cautious whenever we take risks—anything less than caution is pure arrogance and the basis for a serious fall—but life is so arranged to make risk-taking a necessary part of any kind of success. Even more important, you cannot become who you want to be without taking risks. I have decided for myself, therefore, that big risks should only be taken when my livelihood depends on it. Little risks can be taken for the fun and excitement of them. In either case, there are no rewards without them.

CHAPTER 7

Success and Power Fall to Those Who Specialize

Be not afraid of going slowly;
be afraid of standing still
                    —Ancient Chinese proverb

There is an old story about the great artist Pablo Picasso who was sitting in a cafe one afternoon in Paris when he was approached by an American tourist. The woman asked Picasso if he could make a small drawing for her. "I'd be so grateful," the woman said. "And I would pay you, of course." Picasso accepted the piece of paper the woman handed him and then with that extreme concentration that was so characteristic of him, proceeded to create a small drawing. When he was finished, he handed it to the woman.

"Oh, Mr. Picasso, that's beautiful. It's so beautiful," she said. "What do I owe you?"

Picasso smiled and said, "That will be $30,000, madam."

The woman was shocked. "Thirty-thousand dollars," she said. "But it only took you a minute."

"Madam, you're not paying me for the minute it took me to do that drawing," Picasso replied. "You're paying me for the forty years it took me to be able to make such a drawing in a minute."

In that little story lie a great many secrets to success in your career. Picasso did one thing better than just about everyone else: He painted pictures. Because he limited himself to a single area of life, an area in which he had enormous God-given talent, he was able to develop and command his abilities. But then he went even further: He applied his vision of life to his art and produced a unique artistic expression, one that not only expressed his view, but articulated the unspoken feelings of many thousands of other people. Picasso found his own uniqueness; he nurtured and cultivated it; and then he exploited it to the maximum. In the process, he became the full expression of himself as an artist.

I am not saying that he was a man without significant flaws, but he does serve as a good example of what is possible when you specialize in a single area of life, an area in which you have talent, and then develop that aspect of your being. Great success can follow.

One of the lessons I drum into my students at the institutions where I teach is to specialize and become an expert in some area of their profession. Those who become experts in their fields gain a unique knowledge; they develop their skills; they gain a reputation for excellence; and they accrue power and financial success. People flock to them because they want the best advice, or the best service, or the highest-quality product. When you are in such a position, you can charge significant sums of money for your work. As Picasso said, your price should take into consideration all the years it took to develop your talents and to become a prominent expert in your field.

Everyone, I believe, has a money-making niche. For those who find it early in their careers, that niche can be the source of great excitement and commitment that eventually lead to success. For those who find it later in their careers, it can be the basis for a kind of rebirth in their professional lives, especially when it involves an area the person deeply cares about. No matter when you find your career niche, it is an occasion of great enthusiasm. It's as if a great door suddenly opened, allowing new opportunities to flow to you.

One of the interesting things about a career niche is that many people do not have to change careers at all to find their special place. On the contrary, all they have to do is specialize within their field.

I am a venture capitalist—that's a very general field—but I have specialized in investments in biotechnology, especially as it relates to healthcare. I am, for all practical purposes, an expert in this area. Because of my expertise, I have become known throughout my industry. Therefore, many opportunities from all over the world flow to me. Also, I am able to see opportunities that others would overlook, simply because they don't understand the field; they don't know the disciplines involved, nor the leading people and companies.

Today, I am regularly asked to give lectures and presentations on biotech around the world. Not only am I paid to give these talks, but my travels invariably give me the chance to make business contacts with people in my field from around the world. I cannot begin to tell you how many great opportunities have flowed from these contacts.

The path to such specialization, of course, is education and knowledge. No one has a monopoly on knowledge. Anyone can accrue it. All you need to do is study a particular field with passion and conviction. Apply your knowledge and develop your skills. Attend classes, workshops, and professional symposia; talk to other professionals in your field; read; pursue and apply your knowledge. Every year, I attend at least four major conferences to gain new knowledge from other experts in my field. I also attend graduate-level courses at major universities, such as the Harvard Business School. I am constantly learning from my students. It takes time and effort, yes, but this is what a successful career requires: learning and self-development.

As you gain knowledge and skill, you naturally develop greater self-confidence and self-respect, which will reflect in everything you do. Gradually, you feel your own personal power and authority emerging. You are the one who knows about a given area of your profession. Consequently, you find yourself relying on your own knowledge and creativity. In time, a kind of graduation takes place in which you move from a dependent, almost subservient career level, to a place of greater authority, responsibility, and adulthood. With greater knowledge and expertise, you become your own person. You are able to move more freely from one job to another. You realize that you are much more in control of your career.

THEN WHY DO SO MANY FAIL TO MAKE THIS STEP?

The question is, of course, "Why don't more people do it?" When I present this question to my students and colleagues, I consistently get the same answer: More people would specialize if they knew which area of their professions to focus on.

Yes, that's one layer of the problem, but like an onion, the issue is multi-layered. The next layer down, so to speak, is that people do not know what they truly love and where their talents lie. In the absence of such knowledge, too many people withhold their full commitment to their work. In other words, they don't care enough, and that lack of caring changes every-thing about the job. Everyone would love to feel that the job they have is what they were destined to do, but they don't. And in the absence of that feeling, too many people withhold their commitment to their work. The consequence is that the work itself suffers. What they don't realize is that they suffer even more. By withholding our commitment, we have no hope of succeeding in our work.

This brings me to one of the more important truths in life: We've all got to make something better of the imperfect situa-tions in which we find ourselves. All of us yearn for perfection in all-important areas of life—our work, our loved ones, and ourselves—and yet are forced to make the best of the imper-fections we find. No one's work or job is perfect. I don't think the perfect career or work even exists. Nothing on Earth is per-fect. Why should your job be any different? What matters much more is whether you can transform your job into some-thing that you truly enjoy and can use as a vehicle for self-expression and self-development.

To do that, we must do four things. First, we must care deeply about what we do, whatever that job may be, because it is a reflection of who we are; second, we must learn all we can about our field and develop our skills to their potential; third, we must attempt to move our career toward the things that we care most deeply about; and fourth, we must let the web of life help us. If we do the first three—all of which are more or less under our control—the fourth one, which is not, will offer us a significant opportunity to advance. Oftentimes, that oppor-tunity will arrive as a coincidence that appears unexpectedly and without notice.

Caring is the secret to it all. Caring alone accelerates our evolution and moves us closer to the moment when a life-altering door mysteriously opens. On the other hand, if you don't care about your work, get out as fast as you can. A lack of caring will distort you and all that you do. It will change you in all the wrong ways and ruin your feelings about yourself. Of course, eventually it will get you tossed out of your job, which will be a blessing. Do something you care about and your talents will naturally surface.

At this point, many of my readers are asking themselves, "What do I care about?" It's a great question—an essential question, really, one that we should be asking ourselves on a regular basis. Of course, there are many things in our immediate environment that we care about and even love: our family, friends, relatives. But I'm not talking about looking outside ourselves for the things we love; I'm talking about looking inward. A good way to start looking for the answers is to remember your youth.

REMEMBER WHEN EVERYTHING YOU DID CAME FROM CARING

Usually, our talents and passions arise early in life, though when they do, we rarely notice them as such. Very often, our only clue that an activity is an expression of a special talent is that we enjoy doing it, or experience some deep level of satisfaction. For this reason, I often say that the use of one's talent often leads to the experience of joy.

For reasons that I do not fully understand, those things that come from our souls tend to emerge more frequently when we are young. By young, I mean any time during childhood, adolescence, and even our teen years. Maybe it's because, in youth, we do things more for the sheer fun of it—we want to play—rather than out of any sense of responsibility or duty. In our youth, we act more from instinct, and less from any sense of rules and expectations. Even those activities that to others seem like work—such as practicing a musical instrument, studying a particular subject, starting a business, or working endlessly on some form of art—are for you more pleasure than pain. In any case, I believe that the first hints of talent, joy, and passion emerge early in life, or are connected to experiences we have early in life—both good and bad.

While I was a teenager I loved to run, but when I was in high school I hurt my knees and required two operations. One of those operations occurred when I was 17. After the surgery, I was forced to wear an orthopedic knee brace for several weeks. The brace was extremely clumsy, but it gave me an idea: I thought that I could develop a knee brace that would relieve the pressure and pain in the knee and even allow me to go on running. The first thing I did was read as much as I could about the knee. Then I researched the existing braces, including the awkward contraption that was on my own knee. Using that information as my base, I designed a new type of brace for people with strained knees and damaged cartilage. I then went out and raised a little venture capital (one of my teachers gave me the money) so that I could have my own brace constructed.

As it turned out, I created a very good brace. I immediately filed for a patent and then sent my plans and my brace off to a major manufacturer that was already making knee braces. It took a couple of months, but I finally received a letter stating that the company, in fact, was interested in my brace, but when they decided to make a prototype, they discovered that they were already in the midst of designing and manufacturing a brace that was very similar to my own. The company's statement might well have been true, but I never believed it. What I really believed was that they had made a few modifications in my design and claimed it as their own. I was young and naive and had yet to develop any real business skills. But that experience taught me several important lessons. The first was that it's not enough to be creative; you have to protect your ideas if you expect to profit from them. The second was that I really enjoyed working in the health and medical field. I also liked business. The whole experience of designing something, patenting it, and then trying to sell it was really fun. It connected me to something inside myself that gave me great pleasure. And even though I may well have been ripped off in the process, I didn't mind at all, because the work itself gave me so much pleasure. Rather than being discouraged by the experience, I was inspired and wanted to do it again.

My experience with my knee brace was pivotal, because it introduced me to an area of business that I deeply enjoyed. It would take many more experiences and the blessings of the web of life for me to ultimately find my way to my current profession, but the web of life was offering me some early clues that would eventually lead to my goal.

Later I took several personality tests, all of which said that my real abilities lay in the medical and business fields. These tests reinforced the feelings that I got from working on my knee brace.

Years passed, I graduated from college, and wound up on Wall Street with E. F. Hutton, where I worked for Art Carine, Jr., then the executive vice president at Hutton, and my immediate boss, Charlie Murphy; both were extremely good and wise men. I was just starting out in my career and Charlie became my mentor. I worked hard as an account executive and was succeeding modestly, but as I said, I was not particularly good at it. Eventually it became clear to me that I wasn't happy in my job, but I didn't know what to do. One day I went to Charlie and asked his advice. I told him that I was thinking of moving to Israel for awhile, but I wasn't sure. What did he think?

"Peter, that's a perfect idea," Charlie said. "Live in Israel for awhile and experience your roots. When you've found yourself, come back to New York and your job will be waiting for you." Charlie's words landed on me as if they were spoken by an angel—an Irish angel. The world suddenly opened up and the possibilities of life seemed endless.

If he had rejected my idea, or threatened to cut me loose after hearing my indecision about my future, I might have dropped the idea of living abroad. At the very least, I would have had much more difficulty making the decision to leave the U.S. for a time. Instead, Charlie eliminated the losses and made it safe for me to go.

And that's what I did. I went to Israel and worked on a kibbutz. At first, I picked oranges and weeded cotton fields between 4 and 11 A.M. After a season of weeding, I was put on the chicken detail, during which I gathered chickens between 2 and 4 A.M. You had to get three of them in each hand and put them into a truck that took them off to be slaughtered. The work had to be done very early in the morning, when the chickens were sleeping, but as soon as one of them started squawking, the others went wild. Gathering chickens was the worst job I had ever had in my life.

While living in Israel, I got to work with people from all over the world. I made friends with people from Fiji, Sweden, Russia, Ethiopia, Argentina, France, and Ecuador. I learned to appreciate and respect people from cultures that were as different from my own as could possibly be imagined. Such an experience made me see my own country with new eyes. Despite all the mistakes our country has made, despite all the violence and racism that has occurred in America, I came to see the United States as the most benevolent country on Earth.

I'm reminded of what Winston Churchill said about government, which pretty much sums up my feelings about America. "Democracy," Churchill said, "is the worst form of government on earth, but it's better than all the rest." My feelings about the United States are similar. I never stopped seeing the flaws in our country, but as far as I'm concerned, it's better than all the rest.

At the same time, I saw beyond culture and nationality to the universality of the human heart. No matter what our respective cultures may be, we are all more alike than we are different. That's the single greatest lesson I have learned from traveling: Cultures may clash but individuals can understand each other and get along, no matter what their respective racial, ethnic, or religious backgrounds may be.

While traveling, I also saw a great deal of suffering, especially when I visited more poverty-stricken countries. Those who suffered the most, it seemed to me, were the people who were both poor and sick. Seeing people living in small hovels who were extremely ill with pneumonia, gangrenous limbs from diabetes, or some other major illness made me realize again that sickness does not discriminate. It doesn't matter who you are, or what your nationality may be, sickness can strike us all. Thus, we are all united by our fundamental need for good health and healthcare.

It was during this two-year period that I reconnected to my passion for working in healthcare. I would have loved to have been a doctor or a scientist who could deal with these problems directly, but my skills lay elsewhere. However, I could join my abilities with my love of medicine to help scientists find cures for serious illnesses, which is how I came to biotech.

In 1986, I came back to E. F. Hutton, and Art Carine and Charlie Murphy gave me my job back. It was under both of these men that E. F. Hutton also paid for my MBA and allowed me to attend classes in the afternoon. I was in my final term in graduate school when our firm was bought out by Shearson Lehman and both Art and Charlie moved on. I wasn't far behind them. Soon I started working with Dr. Lindsay Rosenwald and began to specialize in healthcare and biotechnology.

SOMETIMES OUR ABILITIES ARE STARING US IN THE FACE

One of the more beautiful and revealing things about human beings is that somehow most people find a way to express a talent or ability, even if it's just as a hobby or an avocation. A person has a lifelong interest in photography and finally buys a camera and starts taking photographs, for example. Another has a special ability as a nurse and volunteers to help people who are ill, or old, or handicapped. Still another loves to paint; he or she takes a class and then starts producing beautiful works of art. These abilities arise mysteriously, gently, humbly, almost without notice, except that they produce such pleasure whenever they are performed. Because they arose so mysteriously and without any great announcement, we tend to take them for granted, like so many of the coincidences that change our lives.

For some, these mere pastimes become the basis for successful businesses. Take Papa John's Pizza, for example. As a kid, John Schnatter loved pizza and even learned how to make it. By the time he reached high school, he dreamed of opening not just a pizza shop, but a whole string of them all over the United States. After high school, he went to Ball State College in Indiana and after graduating sold his car for $3,000, which he used to start his company. He called it Papa John's Pizza. In the year 2000, Papa John's was a publicly traded company with sales of more than $620 million.

Sometimes our abilities are so obvious that we dream of doing other things, rather than doing the work that comes naturally to us. Often the work that comes easiest is not so glamorous as those activities that we have some very obvious ability in. That was certainly the case with Stanley Kaplan, who was a born teacher but nonetheless dreamt of being a doctor.

Stanley Kaplan is the famed creator of the Kaplan Educational Centers, which prepare people for entry examinations to colleges and trade, medical, and law schools all over the world.

Stanley was a brilliant student, getting straight A's throughout his high school and college years. At the age of 15, he started tutoring classmates at the James Madison High School in Brooklyn, New York, for 25 cents an hour. He didn't just teach students the standard curriculum, but prepared them as well for the New York State Regents examinations, which every New York student must take to graduate from high school. Kaplan graduated with five scholastic awards.

When he went on to City College, he continued teaching his classmates in every major discipline—including calculus and physics. By the time he was a senior, Stanley was making almost as much money tutoring as his former high school teachers were making in their full-time jobs. Once again, teaching didn't slow his own studies one bit: Stanley was a Phi Beta Kappa student, was given an award for excellence in science, and graduated magna cum laude from City College in three years.

Despite his obvious scholarship and ability to teach, Stanley dreamt of being a doctor. He believed his excellent academic history and bachelor of science degree would easily get him into medical school. It didn't work out that way, however. In the days before World War II, medical schools had quotas on how many Jews could be accepted each year. Kaplan was both a Jew and a graduate of City College, then a haven for under-privileged New York City residents of every ethnicity, especially African-Americans and Jews.

"Most people are crestfallen when they're rebuffed," Kaplan told a reporter many years later. "But I was kind of glad. I knew I had an alternative. I loved to teach, but I didn't want to be part of the school system. I wanted to use my own methods and develop my own programs." As he would later say, "I was rejected by medical school to invent an industry." Indeed, having nothing else but his love of teaching to fall back on, Stanley Kaplan invented a multimillion-dollar educational business.

Kaplan got a big boost when G.I.s returned from World War II and wanted to get into colleges and graduate, medical, and law schools. Soon he branched out even further to prepare doctors for licensing tests, accountants for the CPA exams, and lawyers for the bar.

"Students were traveling from all over the country to Brooklyn to enroll in my programs," Kaplan recalled. Eventually, they would come from all over the world.

More than three million doctors, lawyers, scientists, engineers, architects, stockbrokers, and teachers have matriculated at the Kaplan Educational Centers, now in more than 1,000 locations around the world. More than 150,000 people study at those centers, in such far-flung places as China, Saudi Arabia, and Hong Kong.

Stanley Kaplan may have wanted to be a doctor, and might have made a very good one at that, but he was a gifted educator who made a great success of his life. Yes, he was unfairly deprived of going into medicine, but because he maintained a positive spirit, and because he recognized where his true talents were, he followed the path of opportunity that was available to him. As it happened, it was a perfect fit, the marriage of talent and opportunity, which led to great rewards and the full expression of his abilities.

MASTER THE BASICS AND THEN DO IT YOUR WAY

No matter who you are, you must learn the basics of your profession in order to succeed. In traditional times, those who showed an aptitude for an art or craft signed on as an apprentice with a master tradesman. The neophyte studied at the foot of the master for many years. In the process, he went through various stages of development, from apprentice to craftsman to journeyman to master. It wasn't until he was a master that he was able to begin to do things the way he saw fit. Until that time, he conducted his profession in the way his forebears had done.

Virtually all of us must follow the same passages of development. Yes, there is the occasional prodigy who appears on the scene and does things uniquely from the beginning. But how many of us are Mozart? Even Picasso had to master the techniques of his art before he began to express his own unique view of life.

My point is that if we learn our jobs thoroughly and master our own skills, we will eventually emerge as a master within our profession. Once we have reached that level, we are often confronted with some great opportunity provided by the web of life. At that point, the sky's the limit.

I am reminded of the story of Robert L. Johnson, founder, former chairman, and former CEO of Black Entertainment Television (BET). Johnson, who turned 54 in the year 2001, was the ninth of ten children. He didn't have very much growing up, except intelligence, ambition, and a winning personality—all he needed to succeed.

Johnson graduated from the University of Illinois and the Woodrow Wilson School of Public and International Affairs at Princeton University. For a short while, he worked for the Corporation for Public Broadcasting and the Urban League, but later got a job as one of the National Cable Television Association's chief lobbyists. Once in his job, Johnson studied the cable TV industry extensively and made a lot of friends.

One day in 1979, Johnson and a colleague were having a discussion about cable television and various segments of the American population. At the time, new networks were arising within the world of cable television, such as CNN and MTV. The colleague said that senior citizens watch a lot of television but feel that they are not portrayed correctly by television.

"You know, the same thing can be said about Black Americans," Johnson said. No sooner had the words come out of his mouth than the idea struck him that a network could be created that was aimed at African-Americans. The idea was pure gold and Johnson knew it. Heck, if MTV and CNN could work, why not a television network designed to provide entertainment to the enormous African-American community?

Johnson went to his longtime friend, John C. Malone, for help in raising the money he needed to start the network. Malone ran TeleCommunications, Inc. (TCI), one of the giant distribution companies that provide cable TV to homes across the nation. Johnson told Malone of his idea and asked him what he could do to help Johnson get the money. Malone, who is white, liked the idea a lot and told Johnson that he would give him $180,000 for 20 percent of Johnson's as yet uncreated enterprise. Johnson was flabbergasted that Malone was so generous and asked for so little in return. "Is that all you want?" Johnson asked Malone. Yes, that was all. In addition, Malone loaned Johnson $320,000, which was the balance of what Johnson needed to start the company. Johnson later said that BET was born because John Malone embraced diversity on television.

BET began airing in 1980 and since then it has prospered beyond anyone's wildest dreams. BET Holdings, the parent company, owns five major cable channels: Black Entertainment Television, which reaches 57.8 million American homes; BET on Jazz: The Jazz Channel, which reaches 2 million U.S. homes and 1 million international subscribers; BET Movies/Starz!, an all-black movie channel; BET Action Pay-per-view, a pay-per-view cable channel that reaches 10 million subscribers; and BET Gospel, founded in December 1998. Johnson has also created BET Pictures II, whose purpose is to create theatrical motion pictures with African-American themes, and BET Arabesque Films, whose purpose is to create made-for-television movies. In addition, BET Holdings also launched several magazines and a restaurant at the Walt Disney World theme park in Orlando.

Today, BET is the only African-American owned and operated company traded on the New York Stock Exchange. In 2000, BET Holdings was sold to Viacom for $3 billion. Even before the sale, Robert Johnson was reported to be worth an estimated $100 million.

That kind of success does not come by thinking exclusively about margins and demographics. It comes by joining the personal with the impersonal. By that I mean, it comes by combining your knowledge of your profession with something unique inside yourself, your own special talents, identity, and your awareness of the needs of others. In Johnson's case, he knew the cable television industry; he had strong business and interpersonal skills; and he knew the needs of the community that he wanted to serve.

He could have remained an executive in that business and achieved a degree of success. But if he had, he would have remained a largely unidentified, almost anonymous figure in a large field. It wasn't until he reached down and expressed more of himself, and found his own identity, that his career realized its potential.

THE GOAL IS TO BRING
FORTH YOURSELF

Sometimes people get the wrong impression when they hear the story of someone who has experienced great success, like that of Robert Johnson. Success comes as a culmination of many small but meaningful experiences. It is the fulfillment of many events, like a series of pearls that combine to create a beautiful necklace. Those small events may be as mundane as learning more about your products or trade, attending courses to increase your knowledge and hone your skills, and improving your ability to communicate your ideas or sell your products.

Sometimes we make the mistake of believing that self-expression must result in some peak experience or big success, but developing your understanding of your career and learning to express yourself in your own unique way is a gradual, unfolding process. You have a chance to emerge from anonymity almost on a daily basis. As you do, you become more identified as an expert in your field.

In 1995, I was asked to give a presentation in Los Angeles before 350 of the wealthiest families in America. The reason for the talk was to introduce investors to our hedgefund, of which I am a fund manager. I was one of 60 speakers that night, all of them managers of major Wall Street funds. Presentations on hedgefunds can be extremely boring, even with the slides, the impressive figures on returns-on-investments, and all those dazzling promises for how much money people will make if they invest in this or that fund. What made matters even worse was that I was the last person to speak that afternoon. I watched people in the room gradually go glassy-eyed, as speaker after speaker went over their hedgefunds in great detail.

"Ugh," I said to myself. "These people are bored senseless. How am I going to get anyone to listen to me? All they can do is think about getting out of here."

I was beside myself as I struggled to figure out how I was going to make my presentation different from all the others. Finally, the speaker before me finished his presentation and our host, Jonathan Brenn, who works for the Hunt family— yes, that Hunt family—introduced me. In his introduction, John made a joke by saying that I was a tough guy, born and bred in Brooklyn, and therefore people had better listen to me. I presumed that it was John's attempt at rousing people from their torpor. "So let's give Peter a nice round of applause," he concluded.

There are a lot of things people might say about me, but "tough" is not among the top four. I can hold the line in nego- tiations as well as anyone, but I believe that I can get a lot more if I preserve everyone's dignity. Very often, I will even give up something that I regard as marginal just so my interlocutor can save face. Yet, John's comment was like an answered prayer. Suddenly, I knew how I was going to talk to these people. But a sudden fear arose inside of me. Do I dare? I wondered. Yes, go ahead, I told myself. Do your Rodney Dangerfield routine. I went to the podium at the front of the room and looked out at the audience.

"John's right, you know," I said. "I am tough. In fact, our neighborhood was so tough that our school newspaper had an obituary section. When I was in elementary school, our teacher asked our class what comes after a sentence and someone yelled out, 'An appeal.' I had an uncle who was a tough guy, too.

Once he asked me if I wanted to go hunting. I told him I was game so he shot me. My wife, she loves to talk during sex, so the other night she called me up from a hotel."

I did eight minutes of Rodney Dangerfield and the people there loved it. Everyone was awake and laughing out loud— thank you, Rodney! Still, I knew that I could not go from Rodney Dangerfield to stocks and bonds, but at that point, I didn't have to. I switched on my projector and went to my last slide. It was a picture of my children.

"You know," I said, there are 59 other great funds to invest in here, and all of them are worth considering, but our fund is the only one that will have a direct impact on your bank account and the health and well-being of your children and grandchildren. Our fund has helped finance more than 100 new drugs for the most serious illnesses facing the world, including breast cancer, prostate cancer, diabetes, AIDS, hemophilia, sickle cell anemia, and genetic illnesses that affect all nationalities. You're not only investing to get a return on your money, but to make a better world for generations to come."

Well, needless to say, that had an impact. After my presentation was over, I was surrounded by people, some who wanted to know more about our fund, others who wanted to invest directly. One of the latter was a Hollywood producer with a long list of blockbusters to his credit.

"I'm not sure what you're selling," he said, "but you've got so much confidence in it that I want to participate. What's your minimum?" A week later, this man deposited $500,000 in our fund.

What would mean even more to my career, however, was another gentleman who came up to me and introduced himself that night. That man was Michael Shimoko, vice president of Sparx Asset Fund Services, Inc., who would become my colleague and collaborator on numerous deals with senior Japanese businessmen. Not only would Michael be an important contact, but he would also become a friend. Through Michael, I met his boss, Mr. Shuhei Abe, founder, president, and CEO of Sparx Asset Management, Co. Ltd., based in Tokyo, with offices in the U.S., Bermuda, and Geneva. Mr. Abe, who formerly managed George Soros's money in Japan, is a man of such integrity and dignity that just to be associated with him is to be given entrée to the upper echelon of the Japanese business world. After I met Mr. Abe, a whole new set of opportunities and business arrangements became available to me, opportunities that changed my life.

I met Michael Shimoko and later, Mr. Abe, because I decided to be myself in a situation in which protocol urged me to be a conformist, to spew forth facts and figures as if I were merely a source of information. Instead, I went the next step— I was a person, with his own personality and his own awareness of the conditions around him. I went from doing what was expected, to doing what I knew to be right—being myself.

THE TRANSFORMATIVE POWER OF YOUR CAREER

I believe that focusing on a specific area of your profession, and in the process gaining extraordinary knowledge and skills, is an essential step in a successful career. It's also an important step in your evolution as a human being. In a way, this is one of the fundamental purposes of life, I believe: to discover and express who you truly are. If we are all the progeny of an infinite Creator, then surely part of our purpose must be to bring forth all the talent and ability that was placed within us. The web of life, it seems to me, provides each of us with our own unique series of lessons, challenges, and opportunities that unfold in time. As we address each of these experiences, honestly and courageously, our talents, abilities, and understanding emerge more clearly.

Gradually, we become the unique creations that we are. That unique being not only has a unique set of skills and experiences, but also a fundamental set of values. Values, as I said in Chapter 2, are what truly separate a successful-and-happy person from one who just makes money. Yes, there are people who get ahead by hurting those they do business with, but they get little or no repeat business and they have to shrink or look away whenever they see old clients. I couldn't live like that.

In a very real sense, your career is a transformative path. In order to develop into the good and successful businessperson you want to become, you must grow as a human being. No matter what your philosophy of life and business may be, you will eventually be defined by how you conducted yourself in business and in life. This is an unavoidable truth about life: Eventually, we all emerge as clearly defined people. Our experiences, expertise, thoughts, emotions, values, and motives shape us so profoundly that we ultimately emerge as well-defined people. In the end, there is no escaping who you really are.

If you specialize in a particular field, you will very likely gain power and success—it's almost unavoidable. What you do with that success and power will determine the kind of person you become. Aim high.

I have examined the lives of many great businesspeople and have witnessed how a personal value or interest—something that sprang from the person's early life—turned out to be the most important factor in the person's success. A. P. Giannini, the founder of Bank of America, is a good example.

Giannini's history reads like the story of George Bailey from the movie *It's a Wonderful Life*. Born in 1870 in San Jose, California, Amadeo Peter Giannini lost his father when he was seven, quit school when he was 14, and went into the produce business with his stepfather. Giannini came from humble people. He grew up in immigrant neighborhoods. These were the people he cared about, the people he wanted to help, if he ever got the chance.

As it turned out, Giannini and his stepfather made a success of their business, largely on A. P.'s reputation for fairness and generosity. When he was 31, A. P. sold his share of the business to his employees and took a seat on the board of directors at Columbus Savings and Loan Society, a small bank in North Beach located in an immigrant Italian neighborhood.

In those days, banks catered exclusively to the rich. Homeowner loans, car loans, and credit to start businesses were all out of reach for the average, hardworking American. Giannini wanted to change all of that. He had come from these people and knew that they could be trusted. These were the people banks should be supporting, he told his fellow board members. Unfortunately, those on the Columbus S&L didn't see things as Giannini did and refused to change their well-established customs. A. P. reacted by quitting the board. He then went out and got ten of his friends, plus his stepfather, to loan him the money to start his own bank, which he opened directly across the street from Columbus S&L. Once his doors opened, A. P. went door-to-door, asking people to deposit their money with him and promising to support them in their dreams for a home, a car, or to start a business.

He loaned money to people whom other banks wouldn't look twice at—average Americans who had a job but, if not helped by banks, would never amass enough money to buy a house. He also supported people who had good ideas for businesses, but had no money to start them. Among them were the families that started the wine industry in northern California. He also backed the motion picture industry; it was his bank's money that was behind the creation of United Artists. He also bailed out Walt Disney when the animator ran $2 million over budget on *Snow White*. In hindsight, these decisions seem like no-brainers, but in the early 1920s, actors, artists, small business people, and common folk were all persona non grata to banks.

Of course, Giannini's bank prospered. He created good karma, you might say. Eventually, he bought other banks, including New York's oldest lending institution, Bank of America. Still, even as his bank grew, he never let go of the guiding principle that made him a success: Loan money to the working-class Americans, whom he was always attempting to make a little richer or more comfortable. One of the ways he did this was by encouraging his employees and depositors to buy shares and own a piece of the bank.

For many years, and particularly in the latter stages of his career, A. P. Giannini worked without pay. When the bank gave him a surprise bonus of $1.5 million, he gave it all to the University of California. When he died at the age of 79, this man, who could have been a billionaire, left an estate worth less than $500,000—and a long legacy of using money to help people who had little of it.

We specialize in our careers and become experts for several reasons: to come to know ourselves and express who we are; to gain authority, influence, and financial success; to support those we love; to make a contribution to our professions and those around us. What better words could be said in anyone's epitaph, but that he used all his abilities, power, and success to make the world a better place.

CHAPTER 8

A User's Guide
to the Web
of Life

A ship in harbor is safe but
that is not what ships are built for
                              —John A. Shedd

*T*he ideas I have tried to put forth in this book represent a way of seeing life. But more important, they are powerful ways to influence others and your environment so that you derive the maximum rewards from life. I have tried to show how coincidence is a sign that indicates the presence of an opportunity; that values nurture opportunity and serve as a compass to success and personal fulfillment; that failure and rejection are temporary but necessary conditions on the path to success; that the courage to leap when the time is right is essential to realizing your heart's desire; that specializing and becoming yourself are the surest paths to power and success. In each of these chapters, I have tried to provide practical guidance. In this chapter, I want to give you easy-to-follow tips for provoking the web of life, so to speak, to act in your favor.

The first thing to say is that we get the most out of the web of life by making positive connections to people and events. By positive connections, I mean the act of providing life-affirming and constructive support to other people and to the situations in which you find yourself. A big part of making the web of life work for you is for you to grow as a human being, to become a richer and fuller person who has the knowledge, maturity, and skill that is needed at the right moment. As I have emphasized, there is absolutely no way around the need to evolve and develop yourself and your skills. But I want to provide tips on how you can do exactly that; to show clearly defined ways that will accelerate your development and increase your opportunities for success.

Here you will find 10 ways to help you do both—to help make your progress in your career more rapid, and to increase the coincidences and opportunities that flow to you. In short, these are 10 ways to pluck the web of life, to make it play for you. Most of these steps can be done by any businessperson at any career level. A few are intended for young people just starting out in their careers and looking for guidance. No doubt, you already will be doing some of the things I recommend— there's no harm in corroborating and supporting you in your efforts. Other recommendations may seem irrelevant to your experience. What I ask is that you try to do as many of the things that I recommend as you can. Meanwhile, search within yourself for your next best step. Sometimes just doing some positive action can stimulate new ideas that would not have come otherwise. One positive action can trigger a series of events that lead to an opportunity that you would never have anticipated. What matters most is that you increase the number of positive connections you make to others and to your work—that every day you are putting out that positive spirit, which inevitably draws forth new opportunities from the web of life.

HERE ARE 10 POSITIVE THINGS YOU CAN DO.

1. Attend Conferences

I go to professional conferences for three reasons. The first is to learn and stay abreast of developments in my profession. I want to know the important trends and where they are headed. One of the best ways to do that is to listen to the leaders of my industry talk about specific areas of our business.

The second reason is to meet people and make important business contacts. Going to conferences is one of the best ways to attract business to my firm, and to meet people who can provide me with new opportunities.

The third is to be inspired. Our lives, and especially our problems, can seem overwhelming at times. A kind of tunnel vision can set in when we live within the narrow confines of our own daily experience. Every now and then, each of us has to do something that breaks us out of that tunnel in order to see our lives in a larger context. Whenever we do that, we can experience gratitude, inspiration, and a larger vision of our lives.

Recently, I attended an investment conference that was attended by the likes of David Rockefeller, Jr. and others of similar status. At that conference I listened to the greatest orator I have ever encountered in my life. His name was Major Charles Plumb, a former Navy pilot who had graduated from the Navy's Top Gun school and was stationed in Vietnam during the war. With less than a month before his discharge, he was shot down and captured by the North Vietnamese. In prison, he joined about 200 other pilots, who, like him, were incarcerated in cells that were 8-feet-square. To illustrate how small his cell was, Major Plumb stood in a square frame of light of the same dimensions that was cast down on him from above the podium. He stood within that light during his entire presentation. The Major spent more than six years in that prison camp, most of which was in that tiny cell.

In addition to the other pilots in prison was a young enlisted Navy seaman. The young man had been scooped out of the water by the North Vietnamese when he fell overboard from his ship that was stationed in the North China Sea. Unlike the others in the prison camp, the seaman had a very different perspective on his imprisonment. As he liked to put it, he wasn't captured, he was rescued. Major Plumb got a good laugh when he showed the audience how differently people can experience the same kinds of conditions.

When the major was shot down, he ejected from the cockpit of his jet and floated safely to Earth, thanks to the fact that his parachute deployed properly. He had been trained to count the panels in the chute to make sure that all of them were opened, lest the thing suddenly collapse and send him hurtling to his death. All the panels opened and as he fell, he silently thanked the young soldier who packed his chute, someone he never knew.

Once he was down on the ground, the major was captured, incarcerated, and tortured in a North Vietnamese prison camp. One of the things he did to keep himself alive was to think about the meals he and his wife would have when he got home. Plumb got married, before leaving for Vietnam. Every day, he thought about the breakfasts, lunches, and dinners he would order when he returned to the U.S. He fantasized about pancakes and eggs—and no rice. Big delicatessen sandwiches and French fries—and no rice. Steaks and potatoes—and no rice. Desserts—but no rice.

The young seaman who was captured with Plumb was released long before the pilots—he did not represent the same kind of power that the Navy flyers did. But while the young man was in prison, he memorized the names, telephone numbers, and addresses of every prisoner in that camp, including Major Plumb's. Once released, the young man crisscrossed the country and visited every family associated with those 200 prisoners. He told each family of the condition of their loved ones and assured them that they were alive and well and eventually would be released. That seaman had been considered the low man on the totem pole in the camp—after all, he held the lowest rank—but his noble act made him the most important to the men of that camp. As the Major told his story, you could hear a pin drop on the carpet of that hotel ballroom. I made a mental note to spend some time with the man who runs our mailroom, because there is no one in any organization who is unimportant.

Eventually, Major Plumb was released. He went home to find that his former wife had left him and married another man. She had waited five years for him, but eventually gave up, met someone else, and married. The major said he understood and went on with his life.

One day when he was sitting in a restaurant in the mid-West, a young man approached him and held out his hand. "Major Plumb?" he asked. The major reached out to shake his hand, but he had to admit he didn't know him. "I'm the guy who packed your parachute the day you were shot down," the young man said. "I hope all the panels opened, sir," the young man said.

In an organization, Major Plumb said, every link in the chain of command is essential. Every person plays a vital role and can be the difference between success and failure—or in the military, between life and death.

Major Plumb's sheer courage, suffering, and endurance ennobled everyone who heard him speak, because he was a living testament to resilience of the human spirit and the heroic potential in all humans. He also managed to put all the problems I had in my life into perspective. After to listening to Major Plumb speak, I felt utterly grateful for my life and every little detail of it.

When the Major stopped speaking, I went over to him and thanked him with all my heart for his inspiration, his sacrifice, and for being the man he was, despite all the challenges that surely would have destroyed a lesser man.

* * *

At another conference, I met and got to spend a few minutes with Mikhail Gorbachev, the former president of the Soviet Union and the man who led the world out of the cold war. Everyone who spoke to Gorbachev was engaging him in a political discussion. Many wanted his thoughts on this subject or that one. Others wanted to give him advice. For my part, I was humbled to meet such a great man; the only thing I could think to do was to tell him a joke. It was slightly off color and very much in the political vein and he loved it. I have a wonderful picture of the two of us together, with him doubled over in laughter.

Another world leader whom I had the pleasure of spending time with at conferences was Alexander Haig, the former Secretary of State and NATO commander-in-chief. General Haig has been a member of the boards of several of the companies of which we are affiliated. I had the pleasure of traveling with him to several business meetings and conferences and had a chance to speak extensively with him. For his work with these companies, he asks only a small honorarium, but takes stock options. If the company succeeds, he succeeds. If it fails, he receives no pay. Once I asked General Haig why he got involved with certain companies. "I only get involved in a company that will have some positive impact on society. If the company succeeds, then I am rewarded, but if it doesn't, I shouldn't be rewarded. It has to be a win-win situation.

"In war," he continued, "you must win. But in peace, relationships have to be win-win situations in order for peace to be maintained."

At another conference, General Haig introduced me to another world leader, Ariel Sharon, the prime minister of Israel. At the conference, I didn't hesitate to tell Sharon how I believed peace could be achieved in the Middle East; how both sides could achieve a win-win situation. It didn't matter whether he agreed with me or not. It was my responsibility as a concerned citizen of the world to press him to act in favor of peace. Besides, it's not as if the leaders there are doing such a great job that they can't use every good idea that people have.

In addition to meeting many inspiring and important figures, such conferences have given me a multitude of business opportunities, as well as the chance to give presentations at major industry gatherings, myself. Conferences are a chance for people with similar business needs to share ideas and resources. These conferences, it seems to me, are the physical manifestations of the web of life within your industry.

2. Take a Course in Public Speaking

Fear of public speaking is the number-one fear among businesspeople in America, followed closely behind, of course, by death. I am reminded of that Jerry Seinfeld joke on the subject. If public speaking is the number-one fear in America, said Seinfeld, that means that the guy giving the eulogy at a funeral would rather be inside the casket than up at the podium.

It's a good idea to videotape yourself as you rehearse your speech. It's a revelation, believe me. So many of the behavior patterns that we take for granted—and would change in an instant—are suddenly visible when we see ourselves on videotape.

If you aspire to be a leader in your profession, you must be a good public speaker. There is no way around it. There are lots of courses in public speaking. Take one. It could be the most important course of your life.

3. Read, Read, Read

Remember the experience of Morris Laster, M.D., whom I wrote about in Chapter 4. Morris helped to found Neose, a company worth more than $600 million, because he read a report in the *Wall Street Journal* about a scientist with a groundbreaking discovery. There are more opportunities in newspapers, magazines, and business reports than any of us will ever be able to realize and exploit. If we only appreciate and develop a tiny fraction of them, we will all be very successful people.

Reading is the basis for understanding people and the world. It opens you up to new ways of thinking, to different cultures and peoples, and to new opportunities that the world is offering, that cannot be discovered in any other way.

In my classes, I encourage every young businessperson to get into the habit of reading *Business Week, Forbes,* and *The Wall Street Journal.* In addition to providing all the latest business news, these periodicals report on new technologies and trends within industries. They also identify the top 100-to-500 fastest growing companies in America, companies that offer new career and investment opportunities.

In addition, I recommend the following ten books as the basis for a better understanding of the business world:

1. *Speaking Secrets of the Masters, by the Speakers Roundtable,* by twenty-two of the World's Top Professional Speakers (Executive Books, 1995). The best advice book on the practice of public speaking, by those who have turned it into an art form. An essential guide for anyone who aspires to high achievement in business.

2. *Patton on Leadership,* by Alan Axelrod (Prentice Hall, 1999). Business and military decision-making have a lot in common. Patton knew when to advance, when to retreat, and when to hold firm. Read this book and learn his secrets. They will guide you far more than you would have ever believed.

3. *Sun Tzu's Art of War for Traders and Investors,* by Dean Lundell (McGraw Hill, 1997). A wonderful guide that

shows how to apply an ancient military philosophy to the subject of managing money and investments.

4. *What They Don't Teach You at Harvard Business School,* by Mark H. McCormack (Bantam Books, 1984). This is a mini-course in business and MBA training. I reread it at least once a year to refresh myself with the ideas.

5. *The Lexus and the Olive Tree,* by Thomas L. Friedman. (Farrar, Straus and Giroux, 1999). A great course in how history and geopolitical decisions are shaping the macro and micro economics of the 21st Century.

6. *Small Miracles,* by Halberstam & Leventhal (Adams Media Corporation, 1997). This book will turn you into a believer. Those who already believe in miracles can experience them.

7. *The Emperors of Chocolate,* by Joel Glenn Brenner (Broadway Books, 1999). A book about the Hershey company and family, one of the great stories of American enterprise. For anyone who wants to really understand competition and the importance of values in the business world.

8. *Tuesdays with Morrie,* by Mitch Albom (Doubleday Books, 1997). I read this book on a cruise while recovering from spinal surgery. Every so often, you need to read something that puts life back into perspective and reminds you of what is really important. This book does exactly that. Moreover, the lessons in this book can be applied to any part of your life, including your career and business.

9. *Life's Little Instruction Book,* by H. Jackson Brown, Jr. (Rutledge Hill Press), 1993. Michael Milken gave me this book and it changed my life. At first, I thought it was just a nice little gift, but after reading it, I understood the message: Be intimate with life and all its many details and rules. It's the basis for living in greater harmony with the earth.

10. *My American Journey,* by Colin L. Powell (Random House, 1995). Wow, a great book by a great leader. Read the last page and realize what a visionary this man really is.

In order to succeed in business, you must be a well-rounded person whose interests extend beyond the business world, into the realms of science, politics, and popular literature.

4. History Matters

There are basically four levels of history: your own personal history; that of your family; your country's history; and world history. We should know something about all four.

The first two histories that you should understand are your own and that of your family. Every family has its traditions, its high points, and—as my own family likes to put it—its mishegus (its craziness). Knowing your family's history is actually an act of honoring your family and yourself. Even if you come from the wackiest or most insane family possible, you should know and understand the story of your family and how you developed within it. Those who know their family histories better understand themselves, their strengths and weaknesses. They also have a better understanding of how those strengths and weaknesses came to be. They have perspective on themselves, and therefore are better able to hold all their many human issues in a more balanced and life-supporting way.

One of the most powerful transformative acts you can do for yourself is to regularly write in a journal or diary. There is good science to show that people who keep journals are better able to resolve long-standing emotional issues and improve their mental health. Keeping a journal serves to document important events and trends in your life; explore your feelings; release pent-up emotions, frustrations, and stress; and to gain an objective look at what you are going through. There are few behaviors, besides exercise and healthy eating, that will do as much for your psychological well-being and self-knowledge as keeping a journal. Keeping a journal, of course, can be seen as recording your own personal history. It is a record of the human drama that you experience, both within and without.

The next two levels of history, of course, are your country's history and world history. One of the great losses of modern culture is that we have avoided knowing the history of our country, even the story of our recent past. I'm more frustrated than amused by Jay Leno's regular feature on the "Tonight" show in which he asks people on the streets of Los Angeles to identify the faces of important government leaders, or to describe events from our recent past. Very few people can identify the most common U.S. and world leaders, and even fewer, it seems, can answer simple questions about our nation's history. We're a country that has lost its past and any sense of our place in world events, which means we do not understand our responsibilities to the future. That's a dangerous situation for any nation to find itself in, but absolutely perilous to the world's leading democracy.

Anyone who travels knows that Europeans and Asians know their own histories, the histories of the world, as well as the history and current events of America. This is not just the intelligentsia of these continents, but the average Luc and Shizuko on the street. Not only do these people know history, but they also know their own folklore, or the mythical stories behind important places and events. For Europeans and Asians, history serves to maintain their traditions and give them a stronger root in their own communities. It grounds them and connects them to each other. I do not mean to suggest that such customs are without their shadows—neither the Europeans nor the Asians are so innovative as Americans—nor do I wish to glorify another country over my own. Just the opposite: If we were to better understand our own history, and that of the world, we would have a greater appreciation for the nation in which we live. We would also know how to better steer its future.

Wherever there is a problem, however, there is also an opportunity. Even though history is often the most neglected subject, it is also one that can most profoundly affect our understanding of the world. Those who have some knowledge of history have a much broader understanding of life. They present themselves as far more educated and capable. They shine in public discussions and are more likely to be perceived as leaders. Indeed, a knowledge of history tends to set people apart from others, making them seem more knowledgeable, wiser, and more capable in many other areas of life.

History teaches us, as well, how others behaved in difficult situations, how their minds worked, what forces drove them to make this decision or that one. History is a great teacher. The people of the past serve as models for how we should or should not behave. They are a source of tremendous inspiration. We are witnesses to great courage, honor, sacrifice, cowardice, betrayal, and lies. It's all there, safely bound between the covers of a book jacket.

There are always history books on the bestsellers list, whether they are the history of an individual, the history of a given period, or an historical novel. The best advice I can give is rather than read broad histories of the world, pick a particular period, or a biography, or the life and times of a particular president, and read a bestseller on the subject, a book of either nonfiction or fiction. I urge people to read at least three books of history per year. In addition, read the newspaper every day, without fail. The newspaper is a daily installment of the world's history—that of your community, your state, your nation, and the world. It will enlarge your life as few other things can.

The irony is that when history is presented in the right way, people love to know about it. A discussion of history always elevates the life condition of all the people who participate in it. People are inspired by a knowledge of history. Those who do not know history, but who listen to such a discussion, automatically tell themselves that they want to better understand history. Why? Because there is something in the human spirit that wants to understand and grasp its own past. We want to understand the behavior of other people and how the current order or disorder in which we live came to be. Try this as an experiment. Read a best-selling history book, remember the details of an important event, or conversation, or battle, and then describe it without pretension but in some detail during your next dinner conversation. Witness how people react. They will be fascinated.

5. Learn a Second Language

This is what I tell every business student I teach or who asks me for advice: Master your business courses and become fluent in a second language. When you graduate, you'll be able to write your own ticket.

The world is getting smaller by the minute. More and more business is international in scope. The next generation of business leaders will be bilingual. Even if you are well beyond the age when learning a second language is customary, take it up as a hobby. Travel to the places where you can use that language. And watch the world open up to you.

The two best languages to learn today—in addition to English, of course—are Spanish and Chinese. These languages will open up the next two big spheres of international business to you. Both the Chinese- and the Spanish-speaking worlds, of course, will become the next two great markets and business powers during the 21st Century. Therefore, those who can communicate in the language of these countries will be in great demand.

6. Set Goals and Realize Them

Set near-term, achievable goals for yourself, as well as goals for one year, three years, and ten years. Write these goals out and indicate how each goal can be achieved. By stating the goal and then saying clearly how it can be achieved, you are actually opening up a path to the realization of your ambitions. In the process of writing out your goals and stating how they can be achieved, you are creating clarity and vision—you are seeing the things you want for your life and how they can be realized.

Be the most clear and definitive about your near-term and one-year ambitions. As you get out to three and ten years, you want to focus more on the big dreams you have and the person you want to become.

Goals are points on a path that lead to the person you want to become. In many cases, they are tangible ambitions: the desire to own a certain car, a house, or have a certain amount of money in the bank. There are goals that help you realize your heart's desire: to have a partner you love, to create a family, to spend more time with the people you love. There are professional goals: the desire to master certain behaviors, to develop certain abilities, to learn more, to get an advanced degree, to change jobs, to be promoted, to start your own business. Many goals are intended to help us develop emotionally, psychologically, and spiritually: to overcome a certain habit or habits, to develop a certain talent, to make peace with a particular person in our lives, to spend more time in quiet contemplation, to attend more spiritual services, to study your own spiritual or religious tradition, to realize greater equanimity and inner peace.

These examples represent a tiny fraction of the limitless number of ambitions people have for their lives. Some people say, "I have no goals." In the vast majority of cases, those who say they have no goals do not know themselves well enough to know what they want or need. They have no idea who they want to become. Their primary goal is to survive, which is not a very high goal, but one that they will achieve, at least for a time. In the meantime, they wander. In order to make the most of your life, you will need goals—even if you don't achieve most of them.

Before you set any goal, focus on what you need, what you want, the circumstances that best support your life, and who you want to become. Let yourself free-associate. Allow yourself to feel and contemplate what you are needing now and then see how those needs connect to your long-term ambitions.

When it comes to setting near-term goals, do not set the bar too high. It will only discourage you if you fail to achieve your aims. Rather, set goals that are significant, meaningful, and important—things that you want to achieve and that will improve your life. By realizing these goals, you will experience your own power to improve your life. Achieving goals is like exercising a muscle—the personal power muscle, you might say. The more goals you achieve, the more you realize how powerful you are to create the kind of life you want to live— and to become the kind of person you want to be.

Think about what your life will be like when these immediate, or near-term, goals are realized.

It often helps to organize your life into major categories— your family, your finances and investments, your professional life, your home, your physical health, your belongings, your emotional-psychological-spiritual existence. Put these categories down into a journal or diary and then make a list of the things you want in each area of your life. Once that is done, organize these ambitions into one-, three-, and ten-year goals.

As much as possible, your goals should line up so that your near-term goals should not only account for your survival, but also help you realize your long-term ambitions.

Goals are your compass in life. They are points of reference by which to set your direction. The thing to remember is that no matter how near-term a goal may be, or how far off it may seem, every goal that you put time and energy into achieving will shape your life for good or ill. In the end, you are created by how you used your time and energy. If you put enough time and energy into a particular ambition, chances are very good that you will get it. But remember the old saying: Be careful what you wish for, because you very well may get it. Another saying of a similar vein is this: More tears have been shed over answered prayers than unanswered ones.

This is one of the primary objectives to setting and achieving near-term goals: You will witness how you create your own life and how you can become the person you want to be.

7. Be Proactive, Not Reactive

When we are in a reactive state, we often feel as if we are victims of larger forces that are overwhelming us. The reason, very simply, is that by the time we address the problem, it has developed into a full-blown crisis. At that point, we must react to it when it has reached its most powerful stage of development. Now you've got a real monster on your hands and it will take a lot more energy and power to defeat it.

Being proactive means addressing an issue directly, actively, with vision and leadership. It also means dealing with problems before they are in a crisis state.

The truth is, there will always be problems and crises no matter how proactive you are. There are two things to say about that: First, be proactive to limit the number of crises you have to face; second, be proactive when it comes to achieving your goals. The fact is that if you are not proactive toward your goals, your chances of achieving them are pretty slim.

8. Collect Business Cards

In your filing cabinet, include files for each profession that you regularly encounter—venture capitalists, traders, fund managers, doctors, lawyers, plumbers, and electricians, as examples—and place the business cards you receive in their respective file, according to profession. When you encounter someone who impresses you and with whom you want to work, include the person in your rolodex, both under his or her name, as well as his or her profession. (I often forget a person's name, but remember after I see or hear it again.)

Of course, make up your own card—even if you are in college—and hand it out whenever appropriate. Business cards are one of the many forms of currency that pass within the web of life.

9. Pick a Sport, Play It Regularly, and Become Good at It

A leader stays physically fit and takes care of his or her body. Your career will demand a great deal from your body. Deadline pressure, long hours of work, endless challenges, disciplining yourself, and travel are just a few of the physical demands you will face. All of these demands create physical tension, which is the basis for most illnesses and addictions. People usually relieve their physical tension by using food, alcohol, drugs, and other forms of addictive behaviors as escape mechanisms. I love good food and a wonderful glass of wine or beer as much as anyone else, but habitual behaviors can destroy your career and your life. The single greatest antidote to these behaviors, I have found, is regular and vigorous exercise.

I swim four or five days a week during my lunch hour. I can get to the pool, swim, shower, and be back in my office in just under an hour. I eat my lunch at my desk. Whenever I travel, I use the gym or health club in my hotel. Exercise is one of the greatest ways to work off jet lag and to remain sharp while you are away from home.

Everyone needs a healthy outlet for his or her tension. The biggest impediment to getting regular exercise, I have found, is that most people do not find a game they enjoy. The consequence is they think of exercise as torture, which is what it feels like if you're not enjoying yourself as you exercise. The only real answer to this is to find a game or a practice that keeps you fit while you work out. The games or practices that can give you pleasure and sustain your fitness include tennis, golf, racquetball, squash, basketball, swimming, and various forms of martial arts, such as Tai Chi (a Chinese form of martial arts that resembles a dance).

It's scientifically well-documented that people who exercise regularly are more likely to live longer and are far less prone to depression and other negative emotional states. As you exercise regularly, you enjoy far greater mental acuity, which of course is fundamental to your success and happiness. You are physically fitter and healthier. You have far more energy and vitality, essential characteristics for leadership.

I mention the physical and mental benefits of exercise first because they are the most important benefits. But it is a fact that certain sports are especially important in business, especially golf, tennis, and racquetball. I knew a guy who was a very good golfer. He had a 2 handicap and was hired over another guy with an MBA from Harvard.

All you need is 20 minutes of aerobic exercise a day. If you are not exercising now, try it and let it change your life.

10. Practice Gratitude

Remember how far you have come, how much you have been given, and who helped you get to where you are. Most of us have faced many, many difficulties in our lives; we've struggled against tremendous odds, and we have come a long way. If you appreciate how hard you have worked and how much you have accomplished, you will look back on your life and be grateful to all who helped you get to where you are. The first step is to truly appreciate yourself and your accomplishments. Gratitude is a natural reaction to such appreciation.

Gratitude helps us relax and appreciate the goodness that is in life and in others. It is the foundation for greater accomplishments and rewards. There can be no real enjoyment of life without appreciation and gratitude. Few things promote positive responses from the web of life like gratitude. People support and elevate those who are grateful. A person who expresses gratitude to you for a service you did him enhances your feelings, not only toward the person himself, but toward the act of service that you did for him. Someone who expresses gratitude to you makes you feel better about yourself. For those who have no gratitude, nothing is good enough and, for such people, all of life is spoiled.

One of the ways to promote gratitude, I believe, is to remember someone in your past who made a difference in your life. For me, the list of people who helped me at crucial times in my life is very long. Some of those people I have written about in this book. But my list of the people I am grateful to begins with one person, my mother. When I think back at how hard she worked so that my two brothers and I had a good start in life, I marvel and am filled with love and gratitude.

After being born in Brooklyn and living there during my early childhood years, we moved to Long Island, where I attended grammar, middle school, and high school. My mother made our lives possible during those years. As hard as my father worked as the family breadwinner and provider, my mother worked even harder. And yet, she never complained, she never bemoaned being a mother. Instead, she loved us with every ounce of energy she had. When I think back to her daily schedule today, I get tired.

HER DAY LOOKED LIKE THIS:

6:15 A.M.   My mother woke up 15 minutes earlier than need be because Dad was in the bathroom playing the radio or showering.

6:30   In morning bathrobe, she set the table and made breakfast for Dad. She also made bagged lunches for her three sons.

6:45   She woke up my brothers Eric and Douglas and me.

7:15   Mother drives Dad to the Long Island Railroad so that he can catch the 7:20 or 7:32 train to Manhattan.

7:30   She returns home, makes sure we've finished breakfast, that we're dressed properly, and that our homework is in order. She gives Eric a dollar for lunch just in case he doesn't eat his peanut butter and jelly sandwich or his Starkist and tomato sandwich.

7:45   I walk to my bus stop after being given my lunch— a sandwich, with a Twinkie or bag of Wise chips.

8:00   Takes kid brother to school or bus stop.

8:15   Showers and then dresses. She drinks her Chock Full of Nuts Coffee and perhaps sneaks a piece of toast on the run.

8:30   Calls her friend Janet Diamond and chats for five minutes as she cleans the table left by Dad and her sons.

8:45   Leaves for work as a bookkeeper.

3:15 P.M.   Arrives back to her "castle"—the word she used for our house—and makes sure her sons have started their homework. She also prepares a snack for us.

4 P.M.   On Mondays and Fridays, my mother brought her sons and their friends to religious school. She did this again on Sunday mornings, at 9 and 11 A.M. All the while, she endured her sons' complaints on the way to religious training.

5 P.M.   Twice a week she takes her sons to piano training. I
             took five years of piano and all I can play today is
             "Heart and Soul." I was so terrible at the piano that
             my father used to pay me not to practice when my
             mother wasn't around and there was something on
             the television that he wanted to watch.

5:30   My mother starts preparing dinner and serves her
             sons. Wednesdays were Prince spaghetti and meat-
             balls with Ragu Tomato sauce (I am not kidding).

6:00   She gets into her car and drives to the train station
             to pick up my father who caught the 6:02 train.
             Sometimes he had to get the later train and could-
             n't call her so she would have to come back, either
             at 6:21 or 6:55. Sometimes my father would fall
             asleep on the train and wake up in Wantagh or
             Massapequa Park! She would have to return to the
             station until he finally woke up and arrived home.
             Somehow she got it right most of the time, which I
             can only attribute to her good intuition.

7:00   She serves Dad dinner and cleans up by 7:30 or 7:40.

7:45   Showers or baths, depending on her mood.

8:15   Makes sure her sons have done their homework.

8:30   She finally gets a chance to relax. She watches the
             Merv Griffin show.

As she watched her show, she did the laundry and ironed.
On Fridays we "helped" her by moving the chairs and table
out of the kitchen so that she could mop the floor. On Saturday
mornings, she vacuumed. My brothers and I mowed the lawn,

raked the leaves, took out the garbage, and shoveled the snow. I still remember how my mother kept us dry during our snowball fights. She put Glad large sandwich bags over our socks before we put our boots on. Afterward, when we came in from the snow, there was plenty of Campbell's Cream of Mushroom soup and Ritz Crackers in the soup.

My mother's work made it possible for every member of our family to do whatever he had to do in life. Her love and hard work served as the center, the very heart, of our family, which was the foundation of our lives.

I will never be able to give back to my mother what she gave to me. Therefore, I live in a perpetual state of gratitude.

EVERYONE HAS SOMEONE TO WHOM THEY ARE GRATEFUL

I believe that there is someone in everyone's life who gave more than he or she could possibly receive in return from us. Moreover, that person's gift to us was essential to each of our lives and our happiness. That person could be a wife, a husband, a brother, sister, uncle, aunt, or friend. Most of us can be grateful to all of these people and many more.

The gifts we have been given place a burden on each of us to make a difference in the lives of others. Our gratitude has to take some active form. Make a difference in the lives of those around you, the people you work with, and those who are below you on the professional totem pole. Add something to their lives. Be that person whom others look back upon and

say, he changed my life, she gave me something I will never forget. And do it because you know that many people have done
the same for you. Such acts not only enrich your life, but make
the web of life work for you.

In this book, I have tried to show you that success, basic
human values, personal development, and a deep sense of fulfillment are not mutually exclusive, but mutually bound
together. They are the basis for success, both professionally and
spiritually. And that, after all, is what we are talking about in
the end. A life well lived is one that unifies earth and heaven,
matter and spirit, survival and love. All of us are dependent
upon each other and upon the mystery that I have loosely, and
somewhat profanely, referred to as the web of life.

Index